Dedicated to those for whom my heart beats—James, Simone and Stephen.

All my love to Mama, Daddy, Angie and Marcus

THE A.G. GASTON MOTEL IN BIRMINGHAM

A Civil Rights Landmark

MARIE A. SUTTON

THE History PRESS

Published by The History Press
Charleston, SC 29403
www.historypress.net

Front cover image, top: Dr. Martin Luther King Jr. and others in the Gaston Motel courtyard. *Courtesy of the Birmingham Public Library*. *Bottom*: The A.G. Gaston Motel. *Courtesy of Chris McNair of Chris McNair Studios.*

First published 2014
Second printing 2015

Manufactured in the United States

ISBN 978.1.62619.595.0

Library of Congress Control Number: 2014951890

CONTENTS

Preface 7
Acknowledgements 9
Introduction 11

1. Locked Out, but Creating a New Way 15
2. A Feather in Birmingham's Cap 25
3. A Place for Us 35
4. Where Trouble Sleeps 42
5. First Class All the Way 52
6. Enough Is Enough 67
7. And a Child Will Lead Them 75
8. The Last Straw 86
9. Music in the Air 96
10. Out of Place 107

Timeline 117
Notes 119
Bibliography 123
Index 125
About the Author 128

PREFACE

For most of my life, I walked around thinking that I knew all there was to know about black history—my history—but what I knew was only a scratch on the surface. Although I was a voracious reader and writer, wrote countless stories about Birmingham and prided myself on being versed in the tales of black struggle and empowerment, it wasn't until I was thirty years old that I learned of Birmingham's full role in the civil rights movement. It wasn't until then that I awakened from a stupor of ignorance and understood the full impact of the bombing of the historic Sixteenth Street Baptist Church, the Children's March and public battles.

For that, I am ashamed.

Little did I know that as a native of Birmingham, Alabama, I had walked the same downtown streets and breathed the same sweet southern air as civil rights icons like Reverends Fred Shuttlesworth, Martin Luther King Jr. and others. I didn't know that my high school alma mater was once for "whites only" and that blacks had to walk past it to attend the one for them, which was farther up the road.

At age thirty, I had the good fortune of working at the Birmingham Civil Rights Institute (BCRI), an educational center devoted to teaching the lessons of the Birmingham movement. When I think about it now, it was divine providence. There, I learned about Birmingham's role in the movement, the names of preachers and common folk, tales of the battles at Kelly Ingram Park and downtown.

After learning about what took place in my city and about the key players who came from where I come from, and who looked like I look, pride swelled within me. I come from the stock of people who braved the wrath of Birmingham's vehement racist Eugene "Bull" Connor, who walked into stinging sheets of water used as a weapon, endured threats of death and braced themselves to be bitten by snarling dogs—all for the right to be considered full-fledged citizens.

As a child, I had heard a little about A.G. Gaston, the black millionaire who provided jobs for countless Birmingham blacks, but I never knew anything about his motel. I didn't know that the A.G. Gaston Motel was the only place blacks could go for first-class accommodations; that iconic black celebrities like Ike and Tina Turner, Ray Charles and the like slept there; and that it was the headquarters for the Birmingham movement. I didn't even know that my own parents had their wedding reception there. Their 1971 Christmas Eve event was all the talk. My afro-clad father and his groomsmen were dressed in tomato red, crushed velvet tuxedos with sea foam green dress shirts, and my waif-thin mother donned a classic satin gown and was surrounded by her smiling bridesmaids while the Gaston served as the backdrop.

When BCRI archivist Laura Anderson mentioned the place to me and told me about its tales and timelines, the storyteller inside me got excited. I wanted to write a book.

At the time, famous art collector Paul R. Jones, who had managed the motel's restaurant during the early 1960s, was coming to Birmingham frequently and agreed to let me interview him for a book. He gave me his phone number and said I was free to come spend time at his house in Atlanta. But I didn't jump on it right away. Then, life happened.

I got married, became pregnant. I got another job and had another baby. Not long after that, Paul Jones died. The idea for the book stalled. Months turned into years. The desire to tell the story, however, never left me. It was like an old debt you know you need to pay; you will not fully rest until it's taken care of.

As my fortieth birthday approached, I made the personal commitment to do it. And when I said "yes," it was as if I became a magnet for information. What once was a nameless, lifeless place on the corner of town came alive to me.

Suddenly, I would hear the motel's name mentioned on television, in lectures and various places. I felt it was confirmation that I am the one who needs to tell the stories.

So I set out on a journey to write about the A.G. Gaston Motel, to venture into the culture and creative spirit of the black race. It became my mission to tell of African Americans who lived, fought and died in Birmingham, Alabama—my home—and how the A.G. Gaston Motel became like a home for activists, celebrities, preachers and common folk when Jim Crow tried to make them homeless.

ACKNOWLEDGEMENTS

For your kind words, swift kicks in the butt, direction, advice, assistance and so much more, I acknowledge you:

Laura Anderson, Dorothy Bailey, Hattie Barnes, Birmingham Civil Rights Institute, Birmingham Public Library, Charles Buchanan, Charla Draper, Andre Elliott, Jimmie Lee Elliott, Marie Elliott, Martez Files, Edna Gardner, Laura Hannah, Tim Hollis, Tamara Harris Johnson, Angela Jones, Marcus Jones, Marlon Jones, Micah Jones, Theresa Jones, Chris McNair, Lisa McNair, Dr. Sarah Parcak, Dr. Robert Smith, Pamela Sterne-King, Amy Sutton, Brenda Sutton, James Sutton Sr. and George A. Washington.

Special thanks to Brenda Jones, who ventured on trips to the library and used her own money to make way too many photocopies for me, who babysat when I needed to write and who constantly offered to help when I did not know what to ask for. I love you.

A big thank you to my dear, sweet daddy: I'll always, always be your number one fan.

Thank you, Kirsten Schofield, Chad Rhoad, Hilary Parrish and The History Press, for giving me a voice (and several extensions).

My eternal gratitude to James, my love: for your prayers, words of encouragement and so much more, I could not have done it without you.

For my life, my words and my everything, I owe it all to you—Jesus.

ACKNOWLEDGEMENTS

For your kind words, swift kicks in the butt, direction, advice, assistance and so much more, I acknowledge you:

Laura Anderson, Dorothy Bailey, Hattie Barnes, Birmingham Civil Rights Institute, Birmingham Public Library, Charles Buchanan, Charla Draper, Andre Elliott, Jimmie Lee Elliott, Marie Elliott, Martez Files, Edna Gardner, Laura Hannah, Tim Hollis, Tamara Harris Johnson, Angela Jones, Marcus Jones, Marlon Jones, Micah Jones, Theresa Jones, Chris McNair, Lisa McNair, Dr. Sarah Parcak, Dr. Robert Smith, Pamela Sterne-King, Amy Sutton, Brenda Sutton, James Sutton Sr. and George A. Washington.

Special thanks to Brenda Jones, who ventured on trips to the library and used her own money to make way too many photocopies for me, who babysat when I needed to write and who constantly offered to help when I did not know what to ask for. I love you.

A big thank you to my dear, sweet daddy: I'll always, always be your number one fan.

Thank you, Kirsten Schofield, Chad Rhoad, Hilary Parrish and The History Press, for giving me a voice (and several extensions).

My eternal gratitude to James, my love: for your prayers, words of encouragement and so much more, I could not have done it without you.

For my life, my words and my everything, I owe it all to you—Jesus.

INTRODUCTION

How does one go about writing a first-of-its-kind book on a topic that is fascinating but piecemeal—commonly known but rarely spoken of? I did not know the answer, but that was my challenge. Boy, was it a challenge.

Although several historical books reference the A.G. Gaston Motel when describing the tumultuous civil rights era in Birmingham, Alabama, there was no one source to go to for comprehensive information. There was only a sentence here, a mention there; a paragraph on this page, a reference on that one.

Many people who would have been adults during its heyday are age eighty and older. Some have died, including the motel's namesake and most of its former staff. The ones who are still living have dim memories. Finding the story seemed to be like looking for a lost penny on an endless, sandy beach.

However, the potential for a story was too good: the parties, the celebrities, the bombing and the tense meetings. The storyteller inside me could not pass it up. So I accepted the challenge with great trepidation.

I had to write about an era that took place before I was born and get information that, I was told, had mostly been destroyed, buried along with the dead or tucked away in some forgotten corner.

The first thing I did was Google the motel's name. Among the list of links, I spotted a video interview that featured the lovely Tamara Harris Johnson. She was the niece of A.G. and Minnie Gaston and agreed to talk to me. Over pancakes at the local International House of Pancakes (sugar-free syrup for her, please), we chatted for hours. She told about the Gastons' nieces and nephews, many of whom are in their fifties and sixties and still remember their uncle Gaston's motel.

Johnson whipped out her cellphone and gave me names and numbers of many folks, a selfless act. One name she gave me was George A. Washington, a suave sixty-something-year-old who had been a regular at the motel almost since it opened back in 1954. He was there to help me narrate its history, the historical and everyday goings-on.

As the story began to come together, another big issue was that no one I had come across had photos of the inside of the motel. I got in touch with Edna Gardner, the matriarch of Minnie Gardner Gaston's family. She is the one who has all the family's pictures, who was always at a relative's event with a camera in tow. She told me that she had several photos of the motel but let someone borrow them and his house had caught fire. I was crushed.

Gardner did come across a gorgeous eight-panel postcard that had artistic renderings of the rooms. It was like striking gold since I had little else. I got a few photos of the motel's exterior from the Birmingham Civil Rights Institute and the Birmingham Public Library and great photos of Gaston himself from Chris McNair, who photographed much of the movement and whose eldest daughter, Denise, was killed in the 1963 bombing of the Sixteenth Street Baptist Church. His wonderful daughter and my friend Lisa McNair was a godsend in getting those.

So, although I was writing about a motel with no photos of the inside, I pressed on because the story was worth telling.

Little things came up and tried to become roadblocks.

I thought I would not ever find out who was the motel's construction company. I called everyone of whom I could think. At the encouragement of Pamela Sterne-King, a dynamic professor at the University of Alabama at Birmingham, I had one of her students help with the search. While he hunted for the information, I checked with BCRI and Urban Impact, a group that serves the interests of Birmingham's historic black business district. No luck. Then, one day: Eureka! As I was on the third floor of the Birmingham Public Library, in the deathly quiet microfilm department, scrolling through issues of *Birmingham World* newspapers, I spotted an article about the grand opening and eyed an ad from the Steel City Construction Company touting that it handled the project.

Then, as I mulled over the list of people I needed to make sure I talk to for the book, a good friend of mine, food writer Charla Draper, mentioned that her friends Ernest and Carolyn Gibson had managed the place. I had never heard of them, so I looked in old issues of *Birmingham World* and saw pictures of their smiling faces. I had struck gold again. They had managed and lived in the motel during its heyday and its most critical times. And, to my delight, they are still alive.

After talking to the Gibsons, Washington and scores of other people, I had to see if their stories lined up chronologically and historically. It was like putting pieces of a puzzle together. Some things overlapped, and some could not be confirmed. A few things had holes, and others seemed too good to be true. I had to research, ask questions and then trust what they said, which can be hard for a former journalist.

After stepping back and looking at the final story, I can only hope that what I found—and I am sure there was much more to find—has been woven into a patchwork of tales and timelines that will resurrect wonderful memories of the motel and do it the justice it deserves.

Chapter 1
LOCKED OUT, BUT CREATING A NEW WAY

I couldn't understand why the color of your skin made you better than me. That didn't make sense.
—Brenda Faush, a native of Birmingham, Alabama

Alabama's scorching summer days do not discriminate. Beneath the merciless sun, there is neither black nor white, rich nor poor—the warmth oppresses all. From the pristine streets of Mountain Brook to the dusty roads of Acipco-Finley, the thick, humid air can be suffocating and the pavement like hot lava.

If your skin is brown, however, it doesn't take long for a million little reminders—like needle-thin icicles—to prick you back into reality; not even the indiscriminate Alabama heat can thaw out cold hearts or melt away the blistering, blue knuckle winter of segregation.

During the 1950s—in the sweltering June, July and August months—a Negro child had to still any excitement at the site of Kiddieland Park.[1] Riding along the endless stretch of Third Avenue West in Birmingham, the fairgrounds could be spotted from the road. The smell of salty, buttered popcorn and sweet, airy cotton candy was a seductive lure. The bright, colorful Ferris wheel sliced through the skyline, and the grounds danced with spinning boxcars, mock airplane rides and a merry-go-round.

Kiddieland was an annual summer carnival that was created in June 1948 for area children. Described by the *Birmingham News*[2] as a "miniature Fairyland," it was touted as "welcome to all," though it was understood that

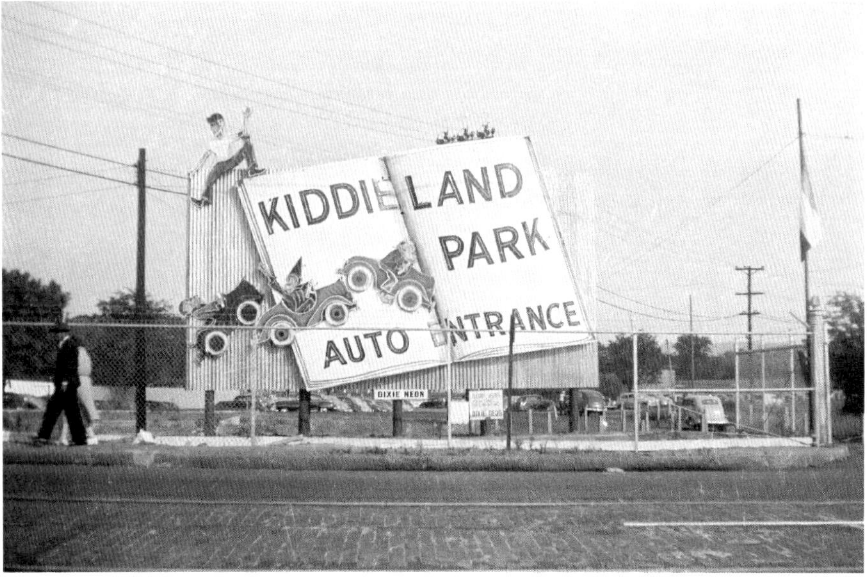

Kiddieland. *Courtesy of Tim Hollis.*

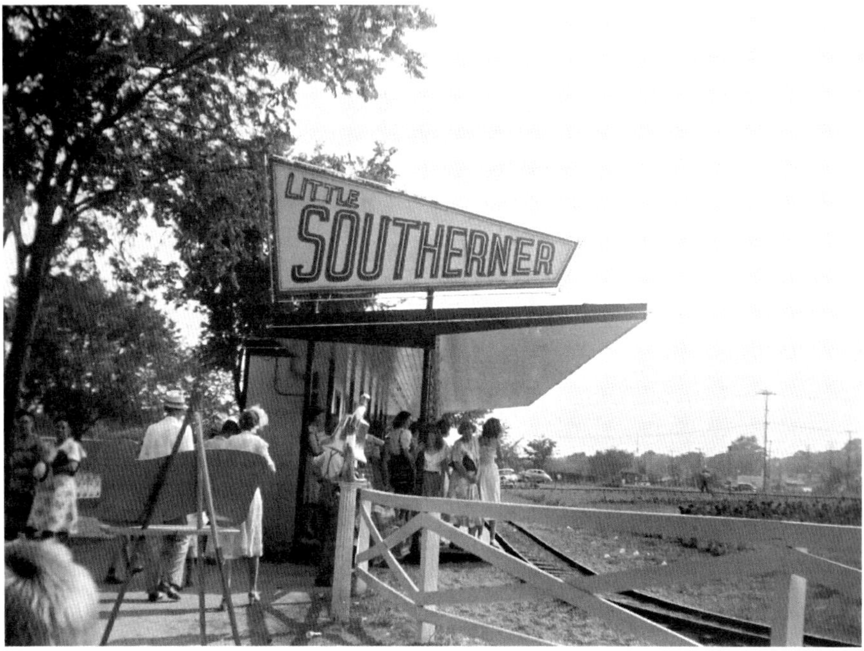

Little Southerner miniature train. *Courtesy of Tim Hollis.*

that meant everyone except Negroes. The fair featured Sunday concerts, "hillbilly" shows, a "pint-sized edition of the Southern Railway's Southerner" train and advertisements that showed rosy-cheeked children drunk with glee. It was not until years later that blacks were allowed to come, but only on the last day when the stuffed toys were usually picked over and nearly gone; the vendors were packing up and the popcorn stale.

Ask a room full of blacks who grew up in Birmingham during that time, and only a scant few won't mention how their memories were stained by not being allowed to attend the fair.

"I remember looking over there and knowing that I couldn't go and not quite understanding why," remembered Samuetta Hill Drew, who was a colored child in Birmingham during the 1950s.

Tamara Harris Johnson's parents tried to shield her from the Kiddieland discussion, she said. Even though the street on which the fair sat was a main artery to downtown, her parents, and many others, found alternative routes so as not to explain why admission to the fair was more than a dime. It also required that your skin be white.

That was the way it was in Birmingham. If you were black, you were only given access to scraps of the American dream; the torn and tattered pieces, the chewed up and spit out ones. Jim Crow laws made sure of it.

City ordinances[3] deemed it illegal for blacks and whites to play cards together or even enjoy movies collectively unless there was separate seating, entrances and exits. And the only way they could eat in the same room was if they were divided by a solid partition that reached at least seven feet from the floor. Signs that read "whites only" hung on doorways and water fountains throughout the city. Even the telephone directories noted whether people or businesses were "C" or "Colored."[4]

At downtown department stores, blacks were not allowed to try on clothes. They had to guess their sizes, buy them off the rack and hope they would fit. If black customers needed new shoes, many would trace their feet on pieces of cardboard at home. Then, at the store, they would hold the board against the bottom soles until they found a match.

Even conventional elevators were off limits. Whites rode the ones in the main area, while the ones in the back were for "niggers and freight."

At the same time, however, blacks built their own communities that were fortified with pride and sustained by unity in spite of outside forces. Smithfield in central Birmingham was the largest black middle-class community.[5] It was populated with affluent and college-educated African Americans. Many were teachers, lawyers, musicians and doctors. They lived in large Colonial

Revival–, Georgian-, Craftsman- or Bungalow-style homes, many of which were designed by Wallace Rayfield. He was the second formally educated and practicing African American architect in the nation at the time and was also a Smithfield resident.

Blacks of every profession lived within blocks of one another, said George A. Washington, who grew up in the area. He remembers a laundry list of them within a stone's throw, including the doctor who lived across the street and did house calls. "We had everything we needed," he said.

Neighborhood children played on manicured lawns in a part of the city that seemed untouched by the crippling Jim Crow. That is, until the Ku Klux Klan planted the occasional bomb, blowing off sides of residences or leveling abodes to smoldering bits; enjoying the Smithfield community came at a price.

In 1947, acclaimed African American civil rights attorney Arthur Davis Shores helped Samuel Matthews, a drill operator, file suit against the city for its racist zoning laws that restricted blacks in where they could live. Matthews had his sights set on living in the all-white North Smithfield. He became the first African American to purchase a home in that area. On his first night there, however, his home was bombed.

Shores continued his fight against the zoning ordinances and, in 1950, successfully filed suit on behalf of Mary Means Monk. The age-old racist ordinance was declared invalid by Judge Clarence Mullins. It was a victory. That same night, though, Monk's home was bombed.[6] Pretty soon, the area got the nickname "Dynamite Hill."

A few miles away, in North Birmingham, sat Collegeville and Acipco-Finley. Many blacks who lived there were blue-collar workers with cracked hands and soft hearts. They lived in an area that sprouted out of housing developed for the employees of Sloss-Sheffield Corporation, Southern Railroad, U.S. Pipe, Jim Walters Corporation and GATX Tank Corporation.[7] Instead of playing among a row of Colonial-style houses, the children in parts of the area played among railyards and old coal cars beneath gray skies laced with sulfur and where the whistle of passing trains filled the air.

They weren't spared the hand of the Klan, either. Their homes, and even churches, were being bombed just like in Smithfield. Nothing a Negro owned or loved was ever not at the mercy of a dynamite-wielding klansman.

Many of the residents of Collegeville, Smithfield and the like worked and owned businesses in the historic Fourth Avenue Business District, which was a thriving, bustling area. Strict segregation laws kept blacks out of certain parts of downtown, and a line of demarcation outlined the area. East of Eighteenth Street North was for whites only, while west of the line toward

Fifteenth Street was for blacks. Every inch of the Fourth Avenue District was populated with black-owned businesses like printing shops, restaurants, beauty salons and law firms. All the parties, shows and social club soirées were likely held somewhere in the area.

The seven-story Colored Masonic Temple was a showpiece in the district. The brick and limestone Renaissance Revival–style building was erected by the black-owned Windham Construction Company and featured a grand ballroom where concerts, dances and society events were held. When the white community invited a big-name African American artist to perform at one of its venues, black promoters would often invite that same artist to stop by the Temple to perform for a crowd of their own people.[8]

A few streets over, the Alabama Penny Savings Bank was a source of pride. It was the first black-owned and operated financial institution in Birmingham and was housed in the six-story brick Pythian Temple that was also constructed by the Windham Company.[9] The bank financed the construction of homes and churches of many blacks during that time, according to the National Historic Register.

During the day, the area swelled with people darting in and out of buildings, doing business, having lunch and making social calls. "It was the hub of the city for African Americans," Drew remembered.

At night, the streets within the district were nearly busting with folks dressed in their Sunday's best. People packed into the Carver and Famous Theaters, as well as countless restaurants, poolrooms and dancehalls, including the Little Savoy Café, which was built in the style of New York's Harlem Savoy Ballroom. The upstairs kitchen produced an endless supply of mouthwatering chicken and steak dinners, and downstairs in the hall you could catch performances by Duke Ellington, Cab Calloway, Lionel Hampton and many others.[10]

"I used to love the way they dressed, like in a movie, like *Harlem Nights*," said Washington, who as a young man would try to go inside the area nightspots. "We would go in, peep in the door and they would put us out."

During that time, the black middle class was growing at a rapid pace. The community roster grew long with names that would later be in history books like Attorney Arthur Shores, famed deejay Shelley "The Playboy" Stewart and business mogul A.G. Gaston. Gaston was a short-statured, chocolate-brown man who had a penchant for dapper dress and a stern business sense.

"He always wore three-piece suits with a little watch chain," wrote civil rights icon and former United States ambassador to the United Nations Andrew Young in his book *An Easy Burden*.[11]

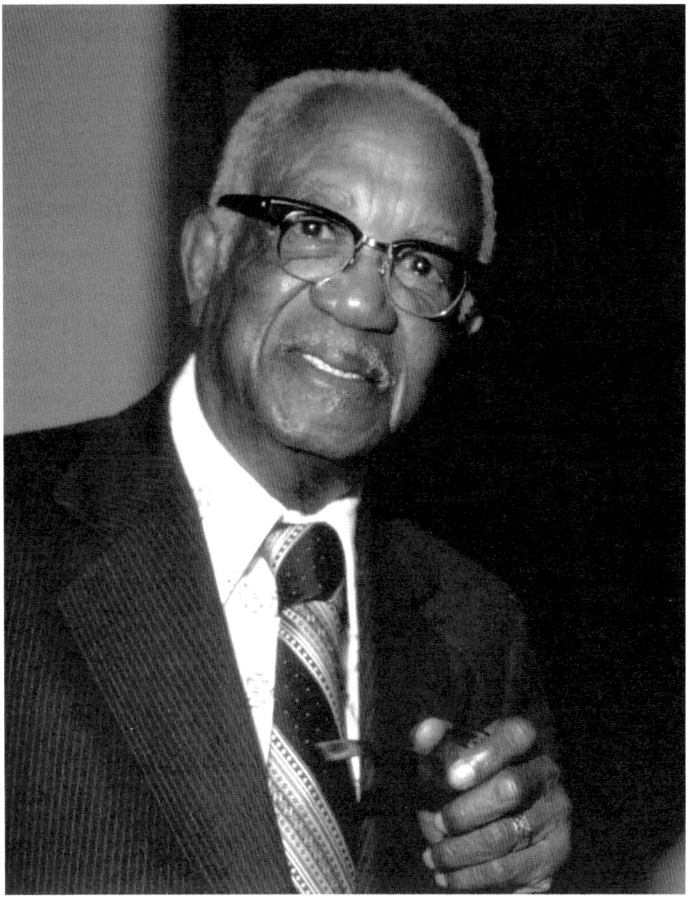

A.G. Gaston. *Photo by Chris McNair of Chris McNair Studios.*

"He was the very image of dignity and wealth," Young wrote, "except for his brown skin."

Gaston, who had only a tenth-grade education,[12] made millions catering to the needs of blacks, a clientele that was often ignored by white business owners. He owned funeral homes, a bank, an insurance company and a radio station; hosted spelling bees for colored children; and founded a girls' and boys' club. He was known for servicing African Americans from the cradle to the grave and advertised his businesses as "strictly 100 percent Negro."[13]

"He was the most powerful man in Birmingham," Washington said. "What he said was the rule of the day, and he generally got what he wanted."

Gaston was born in a log cabin in Demopolis, Alabama, on the Fourth of July 1892. His father, "Papa" as he was known, died seeking work with the Alabama Great Southern Railroad construction project,[11] and his mother, Rosie, was a beloved domestic who cooked and cleaned for A.B. and Minnie Loveman, one of the most affluent white families in the area. The Lovemans owned the popular Loveman, Joseph & Loeb Department Stores.

Born a generation out of slavery, Gaston grew up knowing his place as a black man living in the South. He wrote in his biography, *Green Power*:

> *Any "nigger" who did not jump off the sidewalk when they came by was considered "biggity" by the whole community, and just not well brought up. Most of the civic leaders and professional men were members of the Klan… So, when as a boy I watched a lynching on the street corner, there was no doubt in my mind justice prevailed and that the punishment was surely deserved.*[15]

The Jim Crow way of life did not totally cripple Gaston's family, however. His mother at one time ran a catering business with clients who included some of Birmingham's wealthiest white families.[16] Gaston's grandparents Joe and Idella were born slaves but, after being freed, became business owners who taught him a strong work ethic.

Gaston's first business, down in Demopolis, was selling rides on his family's tire swing. As a young boy, he charged the neighborhood kids a button to ride and ended up with a coffer full.

In 1905, at age thirteen, Gaston moved to Birmingham to be with his mother. She had moved earlier to help the Lovemans relocate to the city. The Lovemans lived in a two-story brick home on the exclusive Rhodes Circle. Gaston and his mother resided in the servants' quarters a short walk away.

Rosie soon enrolled the young boy in the Tuggle Institute, a local boarding school for Negroes who were taught and cared for by Carrie "Granny" Tuggle. The school was located in the middle-class-populated Enon Ridge, which was in north Birmingham. Tuggle was a former slave who had a passion for training up young colored children. She exposed them to the teachings of Booker T. Washington, who was also a former slave turned educator, author and advisor to U.S. presidents. Washington was often a presence on the Tuggle campus and went on to be a major influence on Gaston. His book, *Up from Slavery*, was the first one Gaston read.[17]

When Gaston was older, he began to lay the groundwork for an empire that was built by "filling a need" of the black community. Fresh from fighting the enemy in World War I and back home working among a corps of men in the

Westfield mining village, he and his mother started selling her homemade lunches, many of which consisted of fried chicken, sweet potatoes and flaky biscuits.[18] Then he began making loans to his spend-happy co-workers at a 25 percent interest, which didn't bother him one bit. "In the first place, he was poor, too, and this was merely a way of working to better his own situation. Second, while he had sympathy for the men who were trapped in the mine system, they were not, by and large, his friends."[19]

After a while, Gaston noticed that many black families in his community lacked the means to give their loved ones proper burials. At that time, the mortality rate for blacks in the segregated South was abysmal, and many wanted the memorial services of their loved ones to be special, filled with the pomp and circumstance they never received in this life. A crop of swindlers would supposedly raise funds for dead relatives but were pocketing the profits, Gaston had discovered.

"It was a racket," he was quoted as saying,[20] "and I resented it."

Gaston wanted to remedy this, so he founded a burial society. Members paid him a twenty-five-cent weekly premium for the head of the family and ten cents for each additional member.[21] In the event of their death, they got a first-class funeral.

Locals thought it was a great idea, and the premiums began to come in. But before Gaston could get started good, his first member, Mrs. Sara Emmons, died. He didn't have enough for her funeral. But after much working, negotiating and even prayer, he was able to give the woman a dignified service.

"With a mixture of amazement, joy and relief, I thought, 'Well Brother Gaston, like it or not, it looks like you are in business,'" Gaston wrote.[22]

Tight-fisted with his money and frugal to a fault, Gaston saved enough to expand his reach. After gradual success, he ended up with his own insurance company, then funeral home and next a chain of them. He opened a bank and construction company and even tried his hand at making his own soda.

His first wife and childhood sweetheart, the plump and pretty Creola Smith Gaston, died young right when he was on the cusp of launching his empire. Gaston married his second wife, the lively and beautiful Minnie, in 1943 on the front porch of her sister's New York home.[23] The Tuskegee graduate was a native of rural Lowndes County. She was the fourth of fifteen children and was there by Gaston's side as he grew his enterprises to empire status.

By 1951, Gaston had acquired the largest Negro cemetery in Birmingham—New Grace Hill Cemetery—and then Mason City

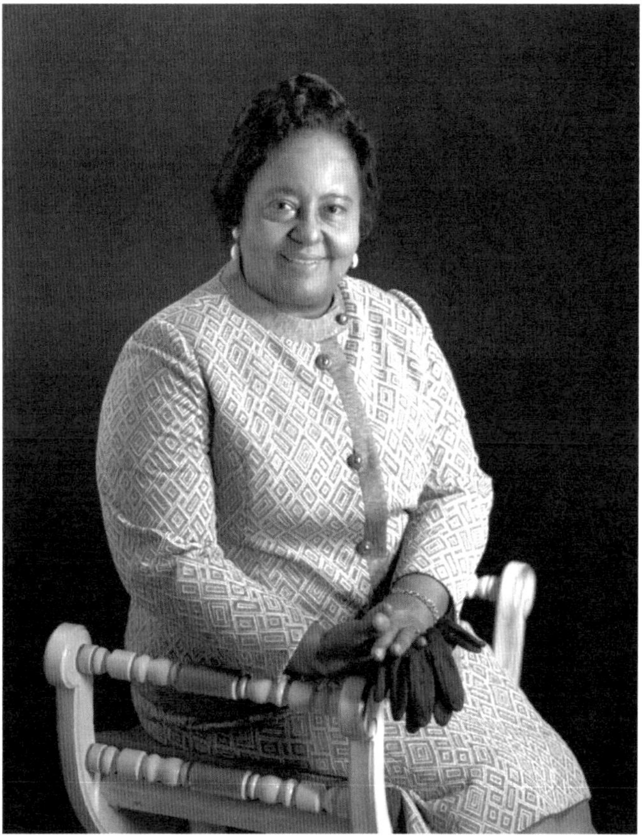

Minnie Gardner. *Photo by Chris McNair of Chris McNair Studios.*

Cemetery.[24] "With the purchase of these sites, Gaston could now control every level of dying, from preparation to interment."[25]

But there was more to him than that, said Reverend Don Solomon, who worked for Gaston for many years. "Dr. Gaston was also a big church man," Solomon, who is a local Baptist preacher, said. He was heavily involved in the African Methodist Episcopal (AME) Church and attended the historic St. John AME Church downtown.

In 1951, Gaston was invited to be the official AME Church delegate to the World Ecumenical Conference in Oxford, England.[26] He was thrilled. The last time Gaston had been in Europe, he was a solider in the army. At that time, the French embraced him and didn't call him a "nigger" or give him limited or no access to their restaurants and stores.

> *In France, he was treated like a man. In France, he could walk the streets without jumping off the sidewalks when a white person strolled by. In France, it was clear, the white people respected his uniform regardless of his color; respected his allegiance to democracy and his willingness to fight for it. In France, it seemed anything was possible for a man like Arthur Gaston.*[27]

When Gaston returned back to Alabama after the war, however, he received the opposite reception in the stiff-necked South. He vowed to visit Europe again, and now he had his chance. The trip to England would prove important in Gaston's legacy, as it would be there that he would stumble upon an idea that would expand his empire and also put him at the center of Birmingham's fight for civil rights, whether he wanted it to or not.

Chapter 2

A FEATHER IN BIRMINGHAM'S CAP

I decided to construct on this land a really fine motel for the Negro citizens of Birmingham.
—A.G. Gaston, owner of the A.G. Gaston Motel

With an invitation to attend the Methodist conference in Oxford, England, Gaston was set to return to Europe. In August 1951, he and Minnie embarked on their journey overseas. They would dock the *Queen Elizabeth* out of New York, and since Minnie had family in the city, she and A.G. spent a few days socializing before setting sail.

In the Big Apple, miles away from the segregated South, Jim Crow didn't restrict the two. The couple stayed at the Waldorf Astoria luxury hotel,[28] though Gaston balked at the pricey rates. Back in Birmingham, Gaston would have been arrested for trying to check into a resort of that caliber. Here, he and his money were welcomed.

Minnie's sister Elizabeth Jenkins and her husband, Edwin, ran the Printing Trades School on Park Avenue South in Manhattan.[29] The couple, as well as other family and friends, fêted the Gastons in high fashion and gave them a bon voyage gala,[30] which was covered by the media and included lots of champagne and well wishes via telegram.

After a high time in New York, the couple docked for England. Inside the boat, they stayed in a lavish stateroom that was adorned with bouquets of blooming flowers and bunches of ripe, colorful fruit.[31] The only other colored family in first class was the Brights, who were diplomats traveling

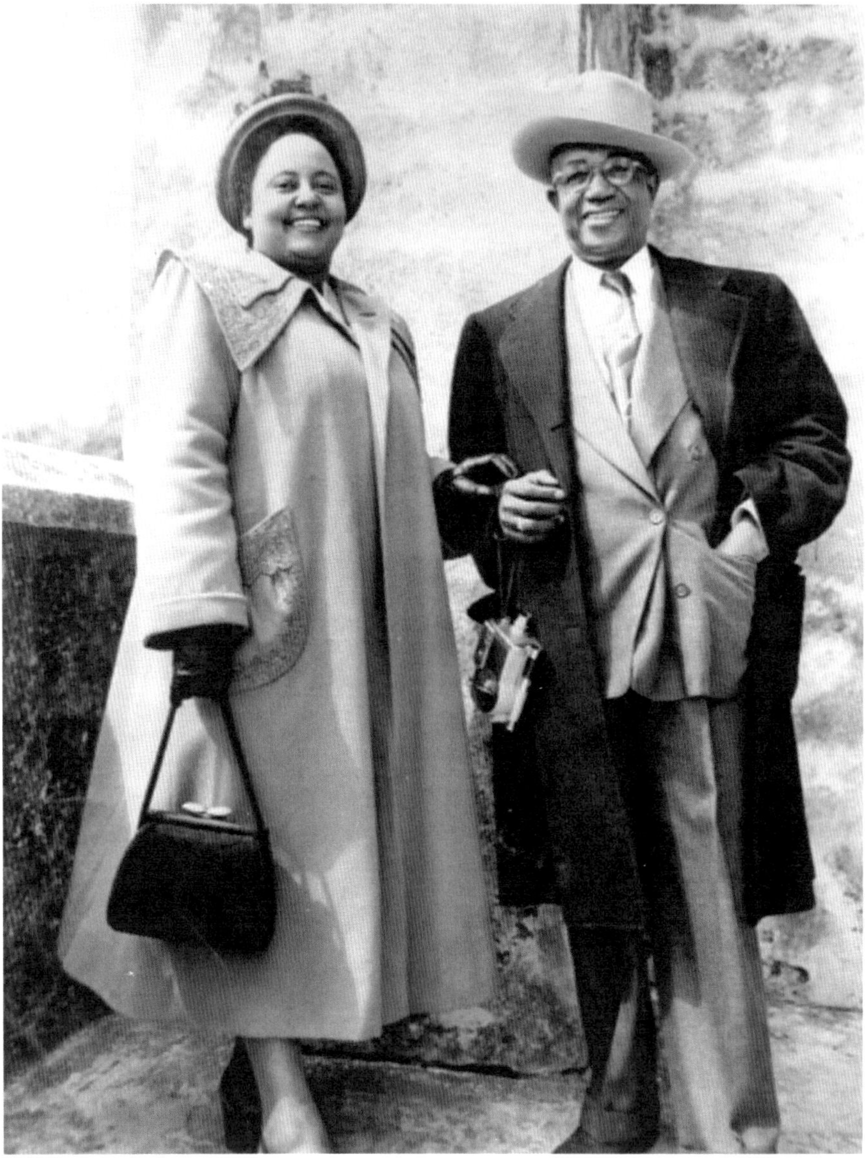

Minnie and A.G. Gaston. *Photo by Chris McNair of Chris McNair Studios.*

back to their home in Liberia, West Africa, after having visited the embassy in Washington.[32]

When the Gastons arrived in London, a chauffeur greeted them and drove them around in a Rolls-Royce that friends from IBM provided for the couple's use. Gaston made full use of his time abroad. He spent hours in the John Wesley room at Lincoln College in Oxford reading the history of the early Methodist Church.[33] He and Minnie also traveled all across Europe, venturing into Buckingham Palace, riding canals in Amsterdam and touring the Holland dikes.[34]

After several trips around town, members of the Scotland Yard, or the local police, began to follow the Gastons, he noted. After some investigating, Gaston learned that locals thought he was famous. They suspected that he was Edmund Anderson, the actor who played the valet Rochester on *The Jack Benny Show*.[35] The police officials thought it wise to follow them in order to provide them with protection.

While at the conference, Gaston got word that the National Sunday School and Baptist Training Union Congress of the National Baptist Convention was considering coming to Birmingham in 1954.[36] With thousands of pastors and parishioners scheduled to attend, this would be one of the largest meetings of its kind to come to the city, according to the black-owned *Birmingham World* newspaper.

This gave Gaston mixed feelings: joy, at the thought of Birmingham being the site for such a great economic opportunity, and disheartenment knowing that blacks would have to struggle to find adequate lodging. The housing issue could jeopardize the group's decision to come, he thought. Gaston saw that as an opportunity to, once again, "fill a need" in the black community.

"I began to consider the accommodations available for such a gathering in Birmingham," he said.[37] "I was proud of the city and had many friends in the Convention…It disturbed me that facilities for Negroes were so limited. White hotels did not accept all races and, with one or two exceptions, the Negro-operated hotels were little more than shelters for transients."

Traveling across the American South with black skin created many inconveniences. You had to arrange lodging with family or church members in the area or take a chance in meager accommodations or boardinghouses. Even Gaston, although he owned millions, could not sleep or eat wherever he wanted below the Mason-Dixon line.

Andrew Young wrote in *An Easy Burden* about hearing a man describe how Gaston drove his big Chrysler to a Chinese restaurant and had to pick up his food at the back door like the other Negroes. "The stinking kitchen door," the man told Young. "And he's the richest black man I ever heard of."[38]

Carolyn McKinstry, who grew up in Birmingham's Thomas area, remembers the pains her family experienced while traveling in the South. Whenever they headed along the highways and byways, they had to pack lunches because they would not be guaranteed to find a restaurant that served blacks.

You only stopped to get gas, she said. Also, when the time would come to use the restroom, it would be challenging. You either had to learn to position yourself near the car for privacy or hope you would see a black person sitting on a porch so that you could ask to use their bathroom, she said.

According to Dr. Thomas Sugrue, professor of history and sociology at the University of Pennsylvania, blacks often "carried buckets or portable toilets in their car trunks" when traveling. Bathrooms and roadside rest areas were off limits to them, he wrote in *Driving While Black: The Car and Race Relations in Modern America*. "Black motorists also found it difficult to find places to stay: most roadside motels—north and south—refused to admit blacks," Sugrue wrote. "Diners and fine restaurants alike regularly turned away black customers."

Out of a great need for information about where blacks could lodge from state to state, *The Negro Traveler's Green Book* was born. Published by Victor H. Green from 1936 to 1964, it was created to help blacks navigate the U.S. roadways.

> *The white traveler has had no difficulty in getting accommodations, but with the Negro it has been different. He, before the advent of a Negro travel guide, had to depend on word of mouth, and many times accommodations were not available.*[39]

The black middle class was growing, and Gaston knew it. Many members of the community were tired of being treated like second-class citizens. They had the desire and the ability to pay for something better.

Whenever an African American celebrity or dignitary came to Birmingham, he would often have to stay with local families who had the means and the extra room to put him up, said Edna Gardner, the matriarch of Minnie Gaston's family. When famed educator and civil rights leader Mary McLeod Bethune came to town, she stayed with the Gastons, as did Supreme Court justice Thurgood Marshall. Baseball great Jackie Robinson had to stay with a family a few doors down, Gardner said.

At the same time, hotels for blacks began popping up in cities across the country. There was the Edward Lee Motel in Jackson, Mississippi; the Sprague Street Hotel in Shreveport, Louisiana; the Lorraine Motel in Memphis, Tennessee; and many others, remembered Shelly Stewart, a wildly popular disc jockey—to white and black listeners—who traveled the country, staying in many of those hotels. Hotels for blacks became a necessity for African American performers, travelers and those with professions that required them to be on the road.

There were hotels that accommodated blacks in Birmingham like the Fraternal Hotel, the Palm Leaf Hotel and Nancy's—all within blocks of one another. And several local nightclub owners, out of necessity, opened roadside inns. The Madison Night Spot on Bessemer Super Highway had an accompanying motel next door. The Grand Terrace Night Club, located in town, had the Grand Terrace Cabins beside it. When entertainers played those clubs, they would stay next door at the inn, Stewart said.

Gaston, though, felt there needed to be a place where people could go in Birmingham for first-class accommodations, where they could experience what he did in New York and England. He wanted to create a motel that had exquisite lodging and fine dining for Negroes.

"That would be a real feather in our town's cap," Gaston wrote in *Green Power*.[10] "As soon as I got home, I would make a little survey of hotel and motel facilities for colored people."

One Journey Ends and Another Begins

After a trip across Europe that included tours of Germany, Monaco, Holland, France and Italy, A.G. and Minnie returned to Birmingham. Minnie came back with a new, pricey five-piece silver service that was purchased from the vaults of England,[11] and A.G. had arrived determined to make his idea for a motel for blacks a reality.

Gaston approached potential investors. They all thought it was a great idea, he said, but provided little more than a handshake and a smile. "There was much talk, which drifted into months, but no financial participation," Gaston wrote.[12] "I decided, as I had been forced to do in the past, to tackle this venture alone."

A lot with a suitable building sat adjacent to his stately white Colonial Smith and Gaston funeral home on the corner of Fifth Avenue and Sixteenth Street North. Gaston acquired the structure, hired architects and financial advisors[13] and sought to renovate it to the tune of $300,000.[14]

"I decided to construct on this land a really fine motel for the Negro citizens of Birmingham," he wrote.[15]

According to Reverend Don Solomon, who worked and climbed the ranks of Gaston's empire until the millionaire died in 1996, Gaston began his research by studying the Holiday Inn, even traveling to Memphis, where the chain was based at the time.

"Gaston tells the story of how he went to talk to the ownership to find out how to build him one," Solomon said. "He built it according to what he learned. As I look back on it, [the Gaston Motel] was almost like the [Holiday Inn] motel, but he put the Gaston swing on it. He spent the big dollar. He went all the way."

Gaston hired Homewood-based Steel City Construction Company to build the two-story brick facility. Stanley B. Echols, a fifty-year-old architect with Brooke B. Burnham, designed the building.

At the same time, in 1953, a young, fiery Baptist preacher with a heartbreaking smile took the helm of Bethel Baptist Church in Collegeville. Reverend Fred L. Shuttlesworth would become the general of the Birmingham civil rights movement, and his church, which "sat in the heart of the industrial Collegeville near iron furnaces and pipe foundries," would be the headquarters.[16] Shuttlesworth's passion for freedom and unrelenting quest for it would cause his paths to cross many times with Gaston and his soon-to-be-built motel.

While construction of the facility continued, Gaston was eyeing a student who was set to graduate from Tuskegee University. He had met Ernest Gibson, a commercial dietetics major, while the young man worked at Tuskegee's Dorothy Hall Guest House. The house was the place dignitaries came for important meetings, etc. In serving Gaston, he and Gibson became good friends.

Gaston wanted the young man to come to Birmingham to work for him at the motel after finishing school. Gibson refused, however, because he had been offered a position with Tuskegee as a junior instructor and had also been drafted to go to Korea. Gaston reluctantly accepted Gibson's refusal but planned to approach him again in the future. George C. Small was hired as the manager to lead the staff.

While the finishing touches and preparation to open the motel's doors were being made, Birmingham residents were celebrating a milestone of national importance. On May 17, 1954, the U.S. Supreme Court ruled in favor of the *Brown v. Board of Education* case, which declared segregated schools unconstitutional. Blacks rejoiced, but local whites rejected the order, and it would soon be apparent that the state and local government would opt to ignore the ruling rather than obey it.

Months later—after countless meetings, tireless days and nights and thousands of dollars spent—Gaston met his goal. The thirty-two-unit, fully

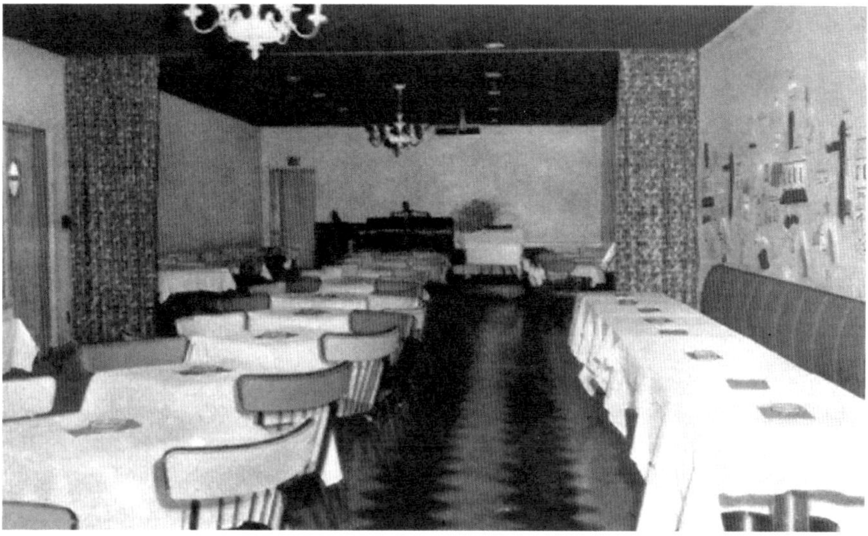

Courtesy of Edna Gardner.

air-conditioned motel opened just in time for the June 22–27, 1954 Baptist convention to converge on the city. The new building sat at 1508–10 Fifth Avenue North. Reservations were available by calling 4-4631.

The *Birmingham News* described the motel as handsomely furnished with a beautiful patio and modern decorations. The drapes and bed coverings were custom-made, and exquisite furniture was purchased from Rhodes Carroll on 2020 Third Avenue North. All the glass was furnished by Uneeda Glass Co. located at 2030 Second Avenue South. Even white hotel operators described it as "one of the finest in the Southeast."

"We just didn't spare any costs in the motel," Gaston told the *News*. "I don't look at it as a business step—but a real adventure in providing something fine that I believe will be appreciated by our people. I am told there is nothing to compare with it anywhere in the world."

Besides the décor, the place was equipped to serve the same mouthwatering food Gaston enjoyed every day. According to Solomon, Gaston brought in his personal chef, Mamie Ruth, to serve as the motel cook. She fashioned the menus and handled all the food, and "it was great," he said.

When the Forty-ninth Session of the National Sunday School and Baptist Training Union Congress arrived in Birmingham, the motel was wall to wall with parishioners and bishops from Atlanta to Oklahoma, from Washington, D.C., to Dallas, Texas.

Ten thousand attendees assembled for the gathering, themed "The Church Fostering Personal Christian Faith in the Home." Registration took place at the historic, all-black A.H. Parker High School, and various venues and churches throughout town served as the sites for the ninety-six courses and six seminars that were taught. Major speakers included Dr. J.H. Jackson, president of the four-million-member National Baptist Convention and pastor of Olivet Baptist Church in Chicago; Reverend Walter Phillip Offutt, church secretary for the National Association for the Advancement of Colored People; and Dr. W.H. Jernagin, celebrated civil rights crusader and president of the congress.

Chairman of the city commission James W. Morgan, Birmingham City Schools superintendent Dr. L. Frazer Banks and several business leaders, including A.G. Gaston, welcomed the group during a ceremony at the Birmingham Municipal Auditorium. According to reporter Richard A. Jackson of the *Birmingham World*, the up-and-coming preacher Dr. Martin Luther King Jr. "exploded" in response to their greetings.

He told the men and the crowd, "The Negro wants his full rights now," and also, "Negroes are not afraid of the white man…Negroes are not interested in marrying white women…that came from the other side of the fence by the whites."

Commissioner Morgan and others stormed off the stage.

Eventually, the smoke cleared, and it was convention business as usual. There was a "mammoth" youth parade Thursday night. The group also passed a resolution to support the recent U.S. Supreme Court ruling against segregation and planned for a Thanksgiving Day pilgrimage to the Lincoln Memorial in Washington, D.C.

The church delegation had cleared out of the city by Sunday, and Gaston readied himself for the official introduction of the motel to the people of Birmingham. In the Wednesday, June 30 issue of the *Birmingham News*, a large display ad posted an invitation for all to the official opening of the A.G. Gaston Motel. It was touted as "The Nation's Newest and Finest Motel for Negroes!"

The amenities listed were:

- Completely air-conditioned
- Gas heat from a central heating system
- Thirty-two units (large and small suites)
- Double and single accommodations
- Spacious lobby
- Completely equipped cafeteria

- Convenient, spacious parking court
- Automatic musical vending device in each unit

Two days later, on Thursday, July 1, Gaston held the official grand opening at 6:30 p.m. The whole community was invited, and the dais was filled with a who's who of black and white Birmingham.

"The new motel serves as a creative symbol spotlighting locally the thrust and possibilities of this raw strength," according to *Birmingham World*, referring to the vast market among the Negroes.

R.A. Hester of Dallas, Texas, who was the supreme chancellor of the Knights of Pythias and was in town for a Lodge Knights of Pythias convention, said it was "the finest hostelry for Negroes in the nation."

The speakers at the opening included Commissioner Morgan; Attorney Shores, who was also chairman of the board of management of the Eighteenth Street Branch YMCA; Mervyn H. Sterne, an investment banker and member of the Birmingham Interracial Committee; Colonel

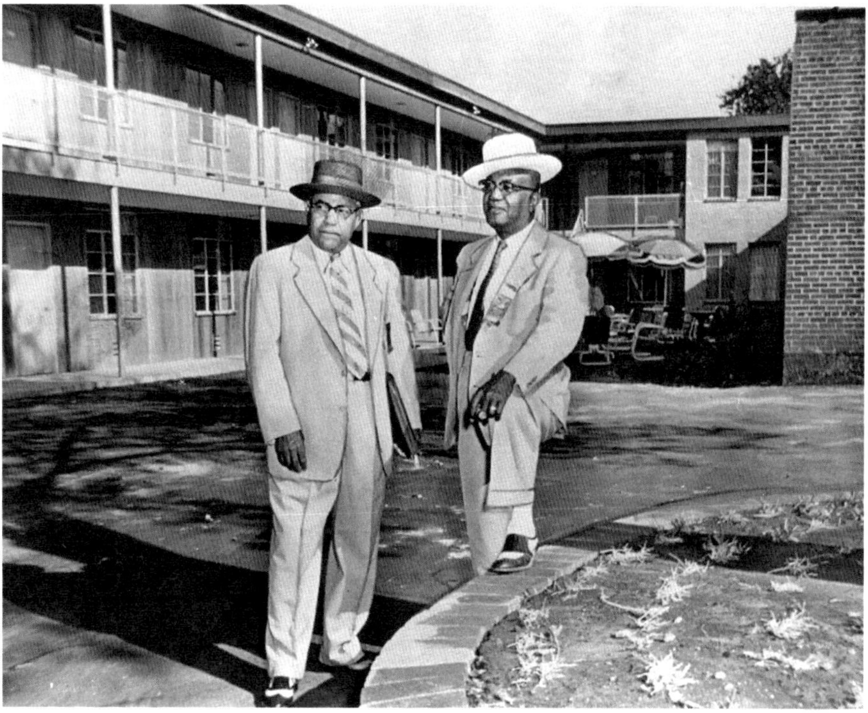

A.G. Gaston and Dallas native R.A. Hester, the supreme chancellor of the Knights of Pythias, stand in the courtyard of the Gaston Motel. *Courtesy of Birmingham Civil Rights Institute.*

Paul Singer, director of the Birmingham Police Department; and Lowell S. Hamilton, president of the Birmingham Chamber of Commerce, among others.

Morgan said Gaston was "the best citizen and best business man of Birmingham," according to *Birmingham World*. He said Gaston "really made his life count."

Morgan also added that Gaston was "a first-class citizen" and that "I'm glad to call him my friend." He said he was proud of the man's achievement and the place he occupied in the favorable growth of the city.

Sterne remarked that there is "no limit to the economic progress you should make."

Shores said that Gaston was one of the giants of business and connected his achievements with improving the general conditions of the Negro group that made possible such progress.

Mrs. Ruth J. Jackson, president of the Birmingham–Jefferson County Housewives League, introduced Gaston, calling him "Birmingham's No. 1 businessman."

When Gaston spoke to the crowd, he thanked "my white and colored friends" for their show of faith and support. He also thanked the platform guests and "other white friends who have aided and encouraged us in this endeavor."

Reverend J.W. Goodgame, pastor of Sixth Avenue Baptist Church, gave the invocation. There were dedicatory expressions given by Miss Alliene Goldsmith, and the occasion was given by L.R. Hall, who presided over the event.

The Booker T. Washington Business College choir, under the direction of W.J. Allen, performed.

By coincidence, said the *Birmingham World* writer, the dedication came the same week a study made by the National Urban League was released showing the improved economic status of Negro workers in the South during the past fifteen years. In addition, *Time* magazine ran a feature on the annual $11 billion Negro market in the United States.

Things were looking up for the Negro, it seemed.

Chapter 3

A PLACE FOR US

Carolyn McKinstry remembers well when the Gaston Motel opened its doors. As a young girl, she heard the adults talk about it and had to see for herself what was inside. One day after Sunday school, she and her friend Junie Collins walked over from Sixteenth Street Baptist Church.

"We sat down and ordered a Coca-Cola, which was a big deal," McKinstry said. It was the first time she had been able to sit down as a colored person and order something in a restaurant without fear of being gawked at or forced to leave.

"It was exhilarating, like we had been given new life," she said. "We could go do what everyone else [white people] could do."

And that Coke.

"That Coke was absolutely wonderful," she said. She mused about the thirty-five-cent beverage that was served with crushed ice in a tall glass and with a straw. "I haven't had a Coke that tasted that good since," she said.

While Gaston's doors were now open to her, all she had known before were doors that were sealed shut. When she walked to school along Finley Avenue West every day, she had to pass by the popular meat-and-three Niki's West Steak and Seafood Restaurant. It did not serve blacks, and her father cautioned her to not even "look like she wanted to eat" there, McKinstry said. Instead, when she neared the tan and brick building, she crossed the street so it would not appear for one second that she wanted to go inside.

The "whites only" restaurants and businesses were like dangling carrots outside the black community's reach. "They put them in the midst of your neighborhood and say, 'You can't go,'" she said.

At Gaston's, though, McKinstry was welcomed and treated with dignity, she said. She felt the Gaston experience was "preparation for what was to come." He primed blacks for what it would feel like to be integrated, she said, to be allowed access to what had been forbidden for many years.

"It was a great place," said Dale Long, whose father, Alexander Long, became the night manager around 1958 until about 1978. The motel, outfitted with a bright, shiny, malt shop and booming jukebox loaded with popular tunes of the day, was appealing to youngsters, he said.

"Kids skipped school to be there," Long said and admitted, "I saw stuff I wasn't supposed to see."

The motel was perfectly sandwiched between the black churches in the community and the place where the youngsters purchased their candy stash. Between 9:00 a.m. Sunday school and 11:00 a.m. church service, the kids from Sixteenth Street Baptist, St. Paul and Metropolitan African Methodist Episcopal Churches would buy penny candy at Citizen's drugstore across the street from the motel. "The drugstore was the meet-up place," Long said. "I would spend my church money." At that time, youth were often in and out of the buildings around that area.

Minnie Gaston, a caramel brown beauty who loved fashion and was always on a diet, never mothered any children of her own. Her nearly five dozen nieces and nephews, however, were like her babies. As a young child, she had a sick mother and a father who worked day in and day out to provide for their large family. She made it her mission to educate her sisters and brothers as well as their children.[17]

Being one of Minnie's "children" meant you had to attend the Booker T. Washington Business College during the summers, whether you were age two or twenty-two. The call went out to the kids who were living everywhere from New York City to up the road in Smithfield. She was the director of the institution, which got its start in 1939 to train blacks in business skills and get them ready for jobs in local businesses, many of which were Gaston enterprises.

Classes included typing, bookkeeping and dictation, among other things. The Gardner kids studied those skills as well as a curriculum divided between the lessons of Booker T. Washington and historian W.E.B. DuBois, with the expectation "that they would become 'The Talented Tenth—who typed.'"[18]

"We all had to go to school," Washington said. "Everybody had to go. You had to do something: typing, math, shorthand. I learned to type and wish I would have taken shorthand."

After a morning of class, the tradition was that at lunchtime the clan of Gardner kids—a rainbow of brown, attractive, well-dressed children, up to a dozen at a time—would walk across the street to the Gaston Motel and order hamburgers, fries and icy Coca-Colas, Washington said. It gave them great pleasure to tell the waitress to "put it on my tab."

Husband-and-wife team Mr. and Mrs. Matthews managed the place at the time. Arzell Skipwith, whom folks called "Skippie," was the cashier at the restaurant. She was out of Birminghamport and had a bright personality; she didn't meet any strangers.

At the end of the day, Minnie would collect the tickets from lunch and pay the bill. That is, until Victor Gardner tried to order a beer, Washington remembered with a hearty laugh. That put an end to that.

The place was a source of pride, and just as if it was his own living room, Gaston would often tweak the décor, Washington remembered. After returning from a safari in Africa, he brought several items to the motel and decked the place with African relics, black cushions, sleek high-backed bar stools and leopard wallpaper. He called it the "Leopard Lounge."

Washington recalled that Gaston "saw those hand drying machines" out west and brought them to the motel. He also had photographs of him and his wife hanging on the walls and added plush booths.

Gaston was a regular at the motel lounge. He and Minnie would come in and sit at the nicest, biggest booth, Washington said. "A.G. would order a bloody rare T-bone steak, salad, burnt toast and a Michelob. That was his regular."

There was much to celebrate with the motel added to the coffer of black businesses in Birmingham. The Gaston Motel was the pride of the community. But still, as long as Jim Crow thrived, there was much to be unsettled about. Although blacks could now experience first-class accommodations at Gaston's, they still could not be treated like full-fledged citizens with access to the same jobs and facilities as others.

In 1955, Shuttlesworth led a petition to demand that the city hire a black policeman.[49] He thought that surely his fellow clergy would be onboard with his effort and sought out the support of the powerful Baptist Ministers' Conference led by Reverend J.L. Ware. The group refused. Ware and Shuttlesworth were rivals. Ware "believed that Shuttlesworth was attempting to usurp his role," wrote Dr. Wilson Fallin in *The African American Church in Birmingham, 1815–1963: A Shelter in the Storm*.[50] Even without them, though,

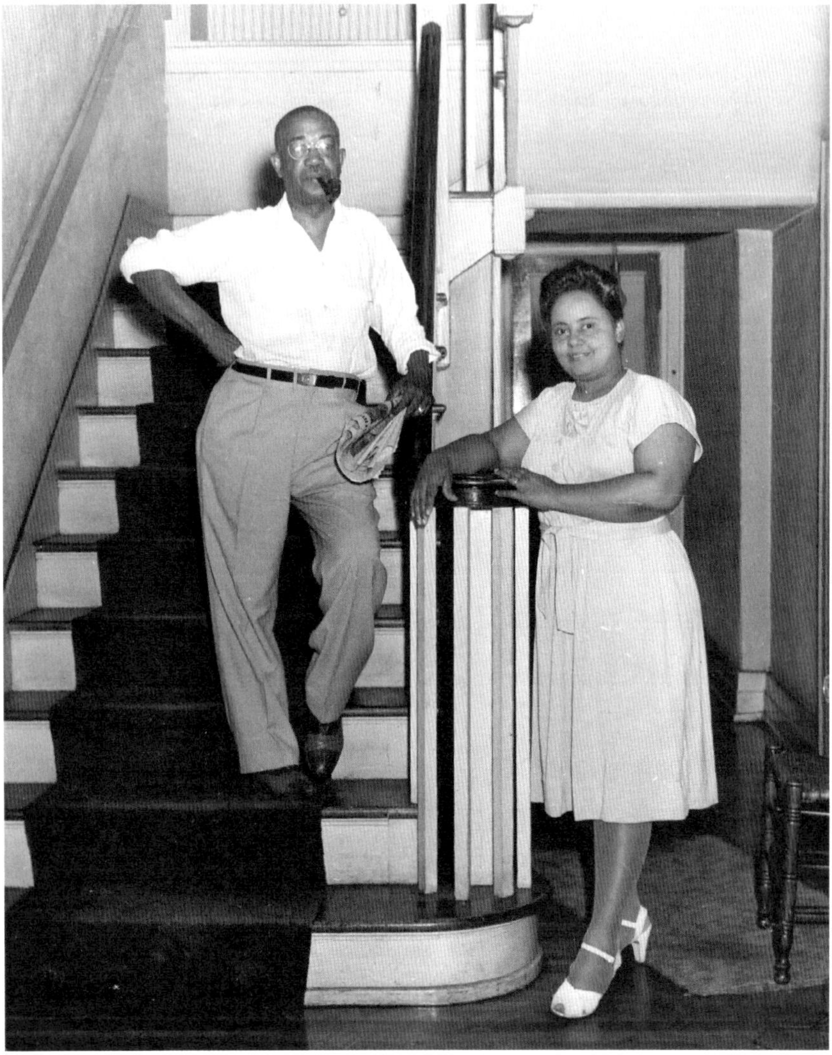

A.G. and Minnie Gaston. *Courtesy of Birmingham Civil Rights Institute.*

Shuttlesworth got close to five thousand signatures and presented the petition to the city commission.

But nothing was ever done, according to historian Dr. Glenn Eskew in *Birmingham Revolutionaries: The Reverend Fred Shuttlesworth and the Alabama Christian Movement for Human Rights*. Soon after the petition, "the lynching of Emmett Till cooled any reformist sympathies in city government and the police force remained all white."[51]

That same year, Autherine Lucy, a young woman from Shiloh, Alabama, along with the National Association for the Advancement of Colored People, won a court order that allowed her and other African American applicants to enroll in the all-white University of Alabama. While engaged in the legal battle, money was tight, so Gaston gave Lucy a job as a secretary at the business college to help with her finances. He was praised as one of her "chief financial backers."[52]

On February 3, 1956, Lucy was able to register at the university. Gaston provided her with "a fine car" from his funeral business.[53] She was scoffed at in the media. They wrote that she was "high-handed"[54] and reported that she appeared for registration well dressed, came in a Cadillac and paid for her tuition in $100 bills.

When she showed up for class, Lucy was mobbed. Her car was pelted with rocks and eggs, which smashed the windows. The crowd yelled, "Let's kill her!" The university suspended Lucy, citing that they could not guarantee her a safe environment.

After that stressful day, Lucy "was whisked to a room in the [Gaston] motel for a little privacy."[55]

But that wasn't the last of the turmoil for Alabama blacks. Later that year, on May 20, 1956, officers padlocked the doors to the local office of the NAACP, Eskew wrote.[56] The state had previously demanded that the organization give over a list of its members, but the group refused. At the time, the national organization had fifty-six branches and fourteen thousand members.[57]

"A state of 'helplessness and hopelessness' descended upon black Birmingham as NAACP members wondered what to do," Eskew wrote.

Shuttlesworth had had enough. He called a mass meeting at Sixteenth Street Baptist Church to discuss the injunction. According to Eskew, one thousand people showed up. At that meeting, the declaration of principles for the Alabama Christian Movement for Human Rights (ACMHR) was announced.[58] Its mission would be to break segregation with boycotts and lawsuits, and Shuttlesworth would be president.

"While Shuttlesworth had expected oppression from white supremacists, he had not anticipated the out and out rejection he and ACMHR received from the black middle class," Eskew wrote.[59] Local perception was that the NAACP members were the "professional people" while the ACMHR "set about organizing the black 'lower class.'"[60]

Shuttlesworth was relatable because he had "played near the ore mines in Oxmoor and whose stepfather was disabled by silicosis."[61] The ACMHR became a network of nearly fifty churches from across the industrial district.

They rotated Monday Mass Meetings, growing the ministry from about three hundred to the thousands.[62] And as they grew, so did the need to have something to meet (and pray) about.

The next year, in September 1957, in retaliation for the desegregation order, the Ku Klux Klan castrated Judge Edward Aaron, a local black man, and poured gasoline on his wounds.[63] During the trial, Theodore Sparks, a Negro, testified on behalf of Klansman Jesse Mabry's character. Sparks said Mabry had a "reputation for truth and veracity." It was thought locally that this had been the first time a black man had testified for the Klan.

By 1959, the ACMHR had about one thousand members.[64] There were mass meetings every Monday at various churches, which included Bethel, New Pilgrim, St. James Baptist, St. John AME and Thirgood CME.[65] With the numbers growing, Shuttlesworth and his ACMHR were assembling an army and bracing themselves for imminent war.

Safety in Numbers

With everything that was going on, the Gastons, whose home would later be bombed more than once, were shaken by the times. Whenever one of them would be out of town, they would invite one of Minnie's young nieces or nephews to stay over for companionship and maybe even protection, Washington said. "I don't know what we could have done," he said with a laugh.

When Minnie was out of town, Gaston would occasionally pick up Washington to be his escort during her absence. On their way to Gaston's home in the Tarrant-Huffman area, the two would make several stops along the way. They would swing by a little convenience store in what was considered the Stockham area because it was near Stockham Valves and Fittings, Washington remembered.

"Go in there and get me a paper and a cigar," Gaston would tell him.

"I'd say, 'OK. Where's the money?'"

"You ain't got no money?" the wealthy Gaston would ask the young boy at the time. "Well, me either," Gaston would say and then drive away rather than crack open his wallet.

The two would often stop by the motel, Washington said, and Gaston would tell him, "Run in there and get us a couple of steaks."

Washington would get a couple of raw T-bones, and then when they got home, he had to make a fire outside on the grill. "He'd throw the two steaks on and three or four pieces of toast," Washington said. "The toast was burnt, and the meat was raw. That's how he liked it."

Gaston would also take a blender and throw in oranges, apples and lemons, churn it all up and pour it into a big glass. He'd devour a dinner of bloody raw steak, burnt toast and a fruit drink concoction. Washington would usually be starving, he said, and would wait to eat until the cook arrived in the morning.

Meanwhile, before heading out of town, Minnie would have given Washington strict instructions not to let her husband go swimming alone. Gaston would get up at 5:00 a.m. and take a dip in the pool.

"He didn't learn to swim until he was about seventy years old," Washington said. "It was cold water. He had a dog paddle he did."

After that, they'd eat breakfast and leave for town around 7:00 a.m. Gaston would stop at his insurance offices around 7:30 a.m. "He would pull up in Fountain Heights, and they'd better be there," Washington said of the staff, "even though the office didn't open to the public until 8:00 or 9:00."

"He might stop at another office and then would get me to school about 8:15," Washington remembered.

Staying with Minnie was a different experience than with A.G., Washington said. Minnie was as sweet as she could be, and totally opposite of the gruff Gaston, he said.

"She would fix dinner and would snack off of everything," according to Washington. "She was always watching her weight. She would eat off of little saucers. She figured the smaller the plate…"

"On Sunday nights, we'd watch TV," he said. "Loretta Young was on. She had a TV show." Young would appear on the TV screen wearing her evening gown, and Minnie would say, "Wait a minute, let me see that gown."

She was sweet but firm, Washington said, and would always caution him, "Don't spend all your time at that motel."

That advice he didn't heed.

Chapter 4

WHERE TROUBLE SLEEPS

Years had passed since the motel's opening, and in 1957, Paul R. Jones, a handsome, peanut butter brown Alabama native who was working as a probation officer with the Jefferson County Juvenile and Domestic Relations Court, found himself riding in a car with A.G. Gaston. The men were part of a group of leaders who had agreed to raise funds for historically black Miles College. After the obligatory pleasantries and chitchat, Gaston approached Jones about managing the restaurant and lounge.

"I've got the motel and the restaurant over here and lounge, and everybody expects me to pay top salaries because of who I am, and I am not over there to run it, and if you are not there, they'll steal you blind," Jones said of Gaston's conversation.

Gaston offered him a job running the motel restaurant, but Jones declined. "A.G., I could never work for you," Jones told him. He then explained that he would want to own the place, not be a worker.

"So he thought about it," Jones said of Gaston. "He and his team got together with me and said, 'OK.'" They picked the date, and Jones put in his thirty-day notice down at the court.[66]

But Jones couldn't have imagined the fallout from his decision, he said. Businessmen from around town who had run-ins with Gaston began to give him warnings.[67] "Do not go into business with A.G. Gaston," Jones was told. "We've all been in business with him…he always wins. He has to win. He needs to win."

Jones felt that his experience would be different because he did not have much to lose. He didn't have to put up any money to go into business with

Gaston, and the restaurant was fully equipped and was operating when he got there, he said.

In a public relations move, the Gaston team announced that it was relinquishing ownership of the restaurant to Jones. Then, Jones stepped up and began to decide what staff would stay and who would have to leave. Soon after, Jones opened the doors under his ownership and called the place Paul's.

Now, those business leaders who had warned him saw the move as a "David and Goliath situation," Jones said. Everyone likes to support the underdog, "so here comes the crowd," Jones said.

On the first day, Jones presented a menu with the restaurant's past staple dishes of southern cuisines but also with additions like chitlins, or small pig intestines. "So on there, instead of just 'chitlins,' I said, put 'Perry County Chitlins' on there [the menu], so all of them could identify with Perry County. Half of them had roots that came from down that way or something."[68]

Open Door Policy

Jones had an open door policy to his restaurant. "You got people coming from north, east and south, west, whites," he said. "I told my folks, I said, 'Serve them.'"

Even some of the officers Jones had known when working at the courts would come in to eat. These were officers who had arrested some of the black customers in the past, he said. "Local people who would come in and see this would half the time order something to go and take it out rather than stay," he said.

Shelley Stewart, the local rock-and-roll deejay who had devoted black and white listeners and also hosted a popular weekly record hop at Don's Teen Town in Bessemer, remembers those days. "The Gaston was where human beings could be accommodated and eat," he said. "Blacks and whites would stay and dine there and enjoy music there. All citizens. We would meet friends there who happened to be white."

Folks would say, "We will meet you at the 'motel,'" Stewart said. "Everyone knew when we said that—whether they be black or white—it meant at the Gaston's. That was the notable thing."

Stewart recalled a time when Patty, a young woman who worked at the radio station with him, inquired about his lunch plans at "the motel."

She was a slim, white woman with long brunette hair, Stewart recalled. He was friends with her father and husband. As a matter of fact, according to Stewart, he had helped her get her job at the station.

"After I would get off the air, I would say, 'I am going down to the motel to have lunch,'" Stewart said. "In time, she said, 'Where are you going?'"

"I said, 'The Gaston Motel.'"

Wanting to experience the Gaston for herself, Patty said, "You wouldn't take me down there. You take my husband, but you won't take me."

Stewart, who drove a 1959 gray Chevy Impala convertible with a black top and red interior, told her to hop in. "The top was down," he said of his automobile. "I drove down Twentieth Street. Patty was sitting in the front seat. She had her shades on, and her hair was blowing in the wind. I had defied Bull Connor, and everyone knew who I was.

"I had gotten down by University Hospital," Stewart recalled. "Now, during that period, the police would be stationed on the corner. I had gotten down by the viaduct and got on First Avenue, and the policeman saw me and started blowing his whistle. *Bllll*…

"I paid him no attention," Stewart said. "Next light, Second Avenue, the policeman was flagging and blowing his whistle. I get down to Fourth Avenue and Twentieth Street, and this policeman got out in front of the car, stopped and had his hands up."

"'What are you doing? Are you Shelley?' he asked.

"'Yes.'

"'Who is this lady?'

"She said, 'I'm Patty. You can ask me.'

"'Shelley, what the…You trying to start a riot?' the officer asked. 'Where y'all going?'

"Patty said, 'We're going to the motel.'

"That's when they called Eugene 'Bull' Connor," Stewart recalled. "I said, 'Follow me to the motel. I am going to have lunch.'

"When I walked in and they saw me with Patty, the folks started to get up and leave," he said. "It would have been OK if it had been a white man."

The staff served Stewart and his guest "right quick," he said. Then they called Gaston and told him all about Stewart's lunch guest. Later on, Gaston said, "Shelley, what you trying to do, get me bombed out here?"

It was common for blacks and whites to eat together at the Gaston, Stewart said, but when the combination was a black man and a white woman, it was scandalous.

Help Is On the Way

Although some blacks and whites were able to break bread together at the Gaston, the racial climate in the city continued to take a nosedive.

Certain local whites still refused to obey the desegregation order, preferring instead to shut down public facilities rather than allow blacks and whites to be together. Seventy-seven parks, thirty-eight playgrounds, eight swimming pools, four golf courses, the zoo, the art museum and the state fair, as well as the municipal auditorium and Legion Field stadium, were shut down instead of opening their doors to all.[69]

But that couldn't last forever. In October 1961, Birmingham judge H.H. Grooms ordered that city pools and parks be desegregated by January 1962 or else.[70]

Sid Smyer, a white man and president of the Birmingham Chamber of Commerce, hoped that there could be a sensible resolution to Groom's order, so the Committee 100 was formed and included every major white business owner and leader in the city. Gaston led Committee 14, a biracial subcommittee of the group. Art Haynes, who succeeded commission chairman James Morgan, thought Gaston would be able to keep the blacks at bay and convince them to accept the Jim Crow way, but he could not and would not.

By then, local college students were preparing to make a statement. From March to June 1962, students from Miles College launched a selective buying campaign. They refused to patronize retailers that adhered to segregation ordinances. The students were joined by peers at Daniel Payne, Birmingham-Southern and Booker T. Washington Business Colleges.

"We would put on our Miles sweaters—purple and gold," remembered Shelley Millender, who was a student at the time. He and his peers would go into the stores, walk around, ride up and down the escalators and make their presence known. All the while, they would hold on to their funds, refusing to patronize the businesses. "We would also go to intimidate black shoppers from buying."

The city did not take lightly to the boycott. On April 3, it cut the surplus food program, which affected mostly poor blacks who depended on that appropriation to eat.

Shuttlesworth wanted to fight back, and he needed backup. He began a campaign to invite Martin Luther King Jr. and his Southern Christian Leadership Conference (SCLC) to Birmingham.

Smyer heard that King was planning to come to town and was not comfortable with that. He formed the Senior Citizens Committee with leading white men who could help solve the race problem before King did it for them.[71] While all the business leaders were meeting regularly to talk about the unrest in the city, Gaston told the committee that they were spinning their wheels if they didn't talk to Shuttlesworth. "I got some money, but that's all," he told them.[72] "Money don't run this thing now. He's the man with the marbles. You have to talk to the marbles."

Days before the planned SCLC convention in Birmingham, Smyer; Roper Dial of Sears, Roebuck & Co.; and Isadore Pizitz of Pizitz met with Gaston, Shuttlesworth and Lucius Pitts, president of Miles College.

Smyer told Shuttlesworth that he did not think the merchants could meet his demands, which included hiring blacks and rejecting racist ordinances. That's all Shuttlesworth needed to hear. He said, "Well, I'm talking to the wrong crowd then. Let's go, gentlemen. Y'all wasting my time. I'm busy. I'm fighting segregation." He left.[73]

On August 22, 1962, almost a month before the planned visit, the Southern Christian Leadership Conference sent out a press release with the heading "SCLC Sets Annual Meet 'In Birmingham'": "We have chosen Birmingham as the site of our annual meeting because it represents the hardcore South, and our affiliate group here has carried on a relentless and sometimes lonely battle for freedom from segregation. We are grateful that some breakthroughs are beginning."

According to the release, the Birmingham convention was expected to be the largest in the SCLC's six-year history. Eight days later, another press statement announced that Dr. W.G. Anderson would receive the inaugural Freedom Award at the forthcoming convention. Anderson, a thirty-four-year-old, led the Albany Movement and had "made the most significant contribution to the nonviolent struggle in the South."

It was also noted that minister and SCLC executive director Wyatt Tee Walker "declined to confirm reports that a major project has been planned for Birmingham, commonly known in civil rights circles as the 'Johannesburg of the South.'"

Walker was then quoted as saying, "I can say that Dr. King has made intensive plans for Alabama during our next program year and Birmingham is in Alabama."

The sixth annual SCLC convention converged in Birmingham on September 25–28, 1962. Three hundred attendees came, including Jackie Robinson and Adam Clayton Powell, with performances by Sammy Davis Jr. Many, if not all, stayed at the Gaston Motel.[74] Shuttlesworth and his ACMHR was the host, and Reverend W. Edmund Gardner, a minister at the local St. John Baptist Church, was the general chairman.

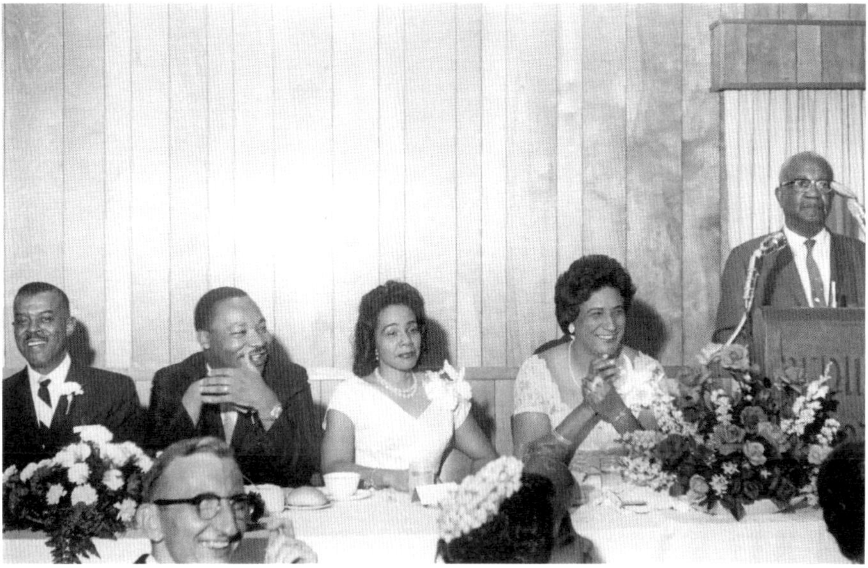

Dr. King and Coretta Scott King at an SCLC event. *Photo by Chris McNair of Chris McNair Studios.*

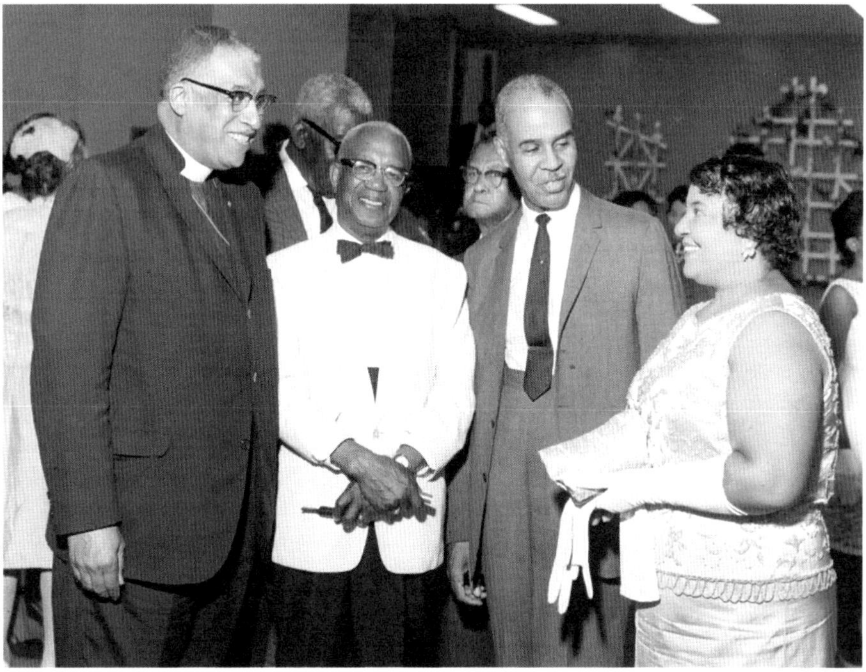

A.G. Gaston with Roy Wilkins and Minnie Gaston. *Photo by Chris McNair of Chris McNair Studios.*

The theme was "Diversified Attack on Segregation," and the headquarters was the Gaston Building's L.R. Hall Auditorium. Registration took place at noon on that Tuesday in the foyer of the building. There was a 2:00 p.m. board meeting at the Metropolitan Baptist Church, and later that night, at 7:00 p.m., a Freedom Dinner served as a tribute to the wives of the freedom fighters. Baseball Hall of Famer Jackie Robinson, who was vice-president in charge of personnel for Chock Full-O-Nuts, gave the address at the wives' tribute dinner.

The SCLC contracted with Paul Jones's restaurant to do the catering, Jones said. "In spite of the fact that we had a mysterious fire in the restaurant that day, we pulled it off without a hitch."

"My restaurant and lounge, and the motel in which they were located, was the only place in town where civil rights activist whites from the north—those helping the SCLC—could stay and eat," Paul Jones was quoted as saying in *Living Art: The Life of Paul R. Jones*.

"Despite segregation ordinances, I fed both blacks and whites without incident and enabled King and his associates to meet with whites coming into Birmingham from all over the country."

"Then, King and other movement leaders moved into the motel and took their meals at my restaurant," Jones said. "They were in and out—Martin

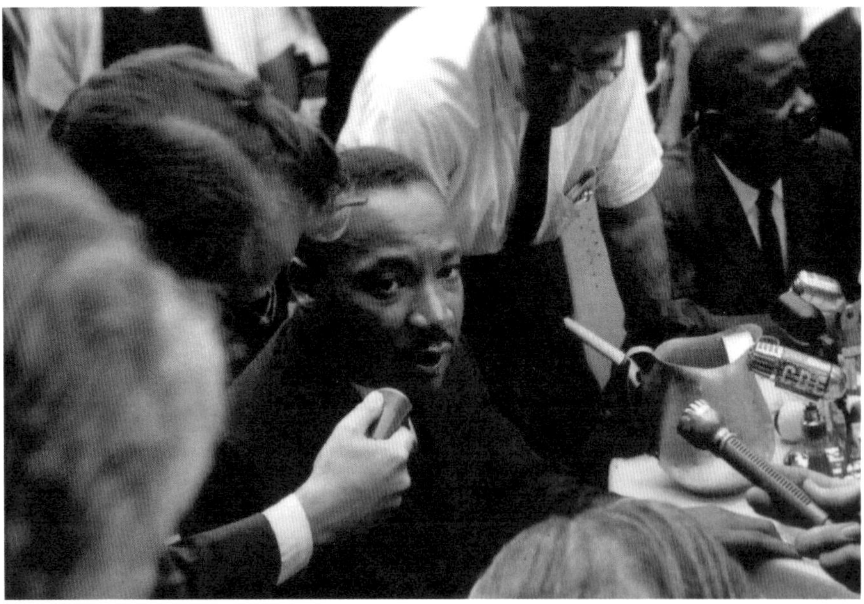

Dr. Martin Luther King Jr. with Reverends Fred L. Shuttlesworth and Ralph Abernathy. *Courtesy of Birmingham Civil Rights Institute.*

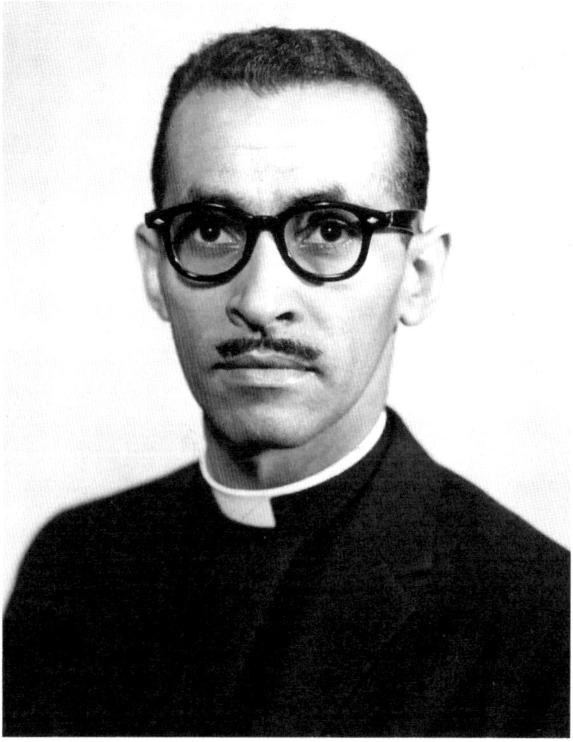

Right: Wyatt Tee Walker, executive director of the Southern Christian Leadership Conference. *Courtesy of Birmingham Civil Rights Institute.*

Below: Andrew Young. *Courtesy of Birmingham Civil Rights Institute.*

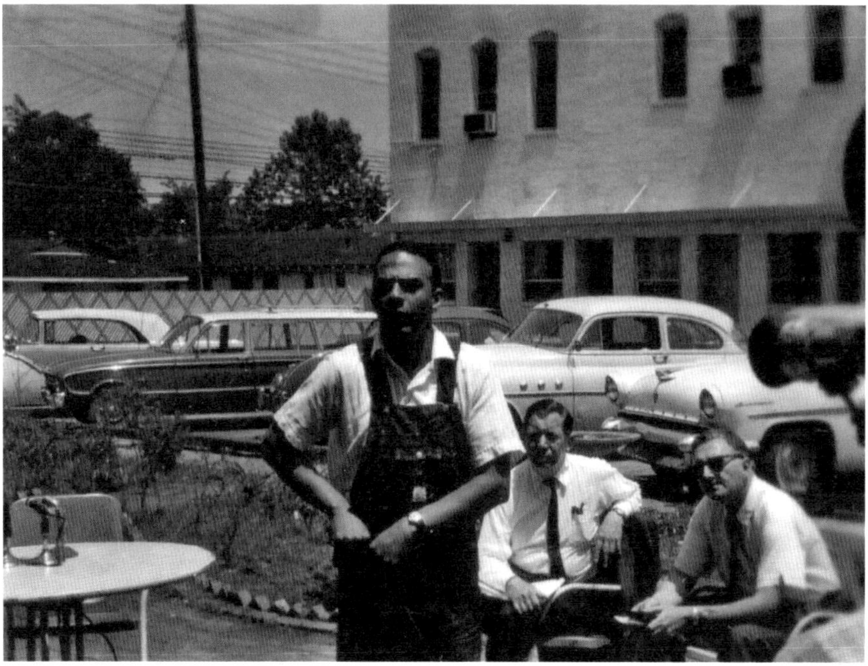

Luther King, Wyatt Tee Walker, Andy Young, Hosea Williams and many others. Some of my regular customers would now order their food to go because of my activist clientele and fear of consequences."

On Wednesday, King gave the 10:00 a.m. formal opening of the annual conference. Among the speakers for that day was Reverend Ralph Abernathy, pastor of West Hunter Street Baptist Church in Atlanta, who gave the 12:15 p.m. keynote address. Others spoke at workshops. That evening, Shuttlesworth hosted an 8:00 p.m. public meeting that included Miles College's Pitts presenting the Rosa Parks Freedom Award to Dr. W.G. Anderson, who was president of the Albany Movement. Parks was there for the presentation of the honor in her name. Following that, the Honorable Adam Clayton Powell (D, NY), chairman of the House Committee on Labor and Education, gave the address.

The next day, there were various sessions and workshops addressing voter registration and direct action, as well as a youth rally led by Miles College student Shelley Millender. That evening, Walker presided over a public meeting at Sixteenth Street Baptist Church. King gave the address.

On the final day, there were business sessions where staff reported efforts in voter registration, citizenship schools, direct action and nonviolent philosophy.

At the same time, there was a change in Birmingham leadership. The three-commissioner government was called into question and went before the people in a vote. Birmingham citizens overturned that long-held government hierarchy in exchange for a mayor-council regime. Eugene "Bull" Connor, a vehement racist and the sitting commissioner for public safety, disputed the results and would not vacate the position. A legal battle was waged, and in the meantime, for almost a year, there were two governments in Birmingham.

Also that year, Gaston's $1.5 million A.G. Gaston Building opened. The three-story, first-rate green and beige building housed his black-owned enterprises and was a center of pride for blacks. Inside were his Booker T. Washington Insurance Company, Citizens Federal Savings and Loan, Vulcan Realty and Investment, Alexander & Company General Insurance and Booker T. Washington Business College. His funeral home moved to Fourth Avenue and Fifteenth Street, and almost immediately, the Townsend family built the Gulf Service Station, one of the only black-owned locations in town. It was a full-service station where you could get your car lubricated, windows washed and air put in your tires. The motel had an entrance right next to the service station. The door led into the lounge, Charles Townsend said. That area of town became a mecca for black businesses.

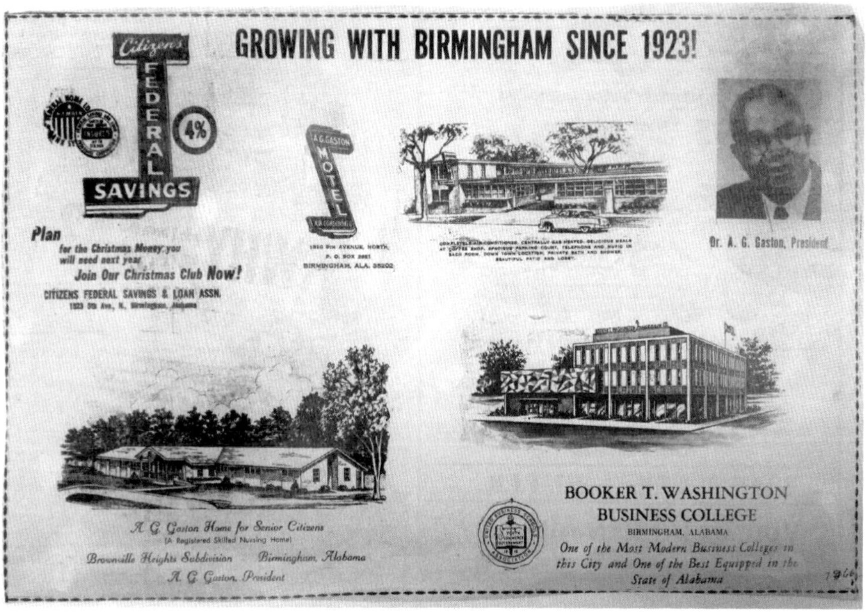

Advertisement for the A.G. Gaston Enterprises. *Courtesy of Birmingham Civil Rights Institute.*

Although running a restaurant was a good opportunity for Paul Jones, he had long wanted a chance to work for the federal courts, he said. As fate would have it, he got a call from the chief probation officer in San Francisco upon the recommendation of a colleague. The man picked Jones to be the first black federal probation officer in that area. Jones headed to California for an opportunity of a lifetime and also to attend the University of California to work on a doctorate degree.[75]

Just like that, he was gone.

Chapter 5

FIRST CLASS ALL THE WAY

In 1963, the Negro, who had realized for many years that he was not truly free, awoke from a stupor of inaction with the cold dash of realization that 1963 meant one hundred years after Lincoln gave his autograph to cause of freedom.
—Martin Luther King Jr., from Why We Can't Wait[76]

After a while, the motel began to show the effects of wear and tear. Paul Jones was gone, and Gaston was not pleased with the way the place was being run. He had envisioned a first-class facility, and it was slipping beneath his dream.

Gaston thought back to that Tuskegee student who gave him impeccable service. He would set out to find him, and this time, he would not take no for an answer.

After Gibson had turned down Gaston back in 1954, the Salem, New Jersey native served in the military for two years. Then, the young man returned to Tuskegee and worked at the university as an instructor. After that, he went to graduate school at Michigan State University to get his master's in hotel and restaurant management.

In 1959, Gibson was hired as the director of food services at Arkansas Agriculture Mechanical and Normal (AM&N) College at Pine Bluff, now the University of Arkansas at Pine Bluff. In his first year, he created a system that got him high praise from campus and state officials. The next year, he was promoted to director of the Student Union and Food Services.

Ernest E. Gibson Named Gaston Lounge Manager

The official announcement was made by Dr. A. G. Gaston, president of Smith and Gaston Interests. Dr. Gaston said Mr. Gibson began his duties Friday, Feb. 1.

Mr. Gibson resigned his position as director of Student Union and Food Services at Arkansas Agricultural, Mechanical and Normal College, Pine Bluff, Ark., Jan. 31, to accept his new post with the Gaston enterprises.

The anouncement added: Because of the nature of the new position accepted by Mr. Gibson, it represents a promotion in that he will become linked with one of the South's oldest and most progressive institutions of its kind.

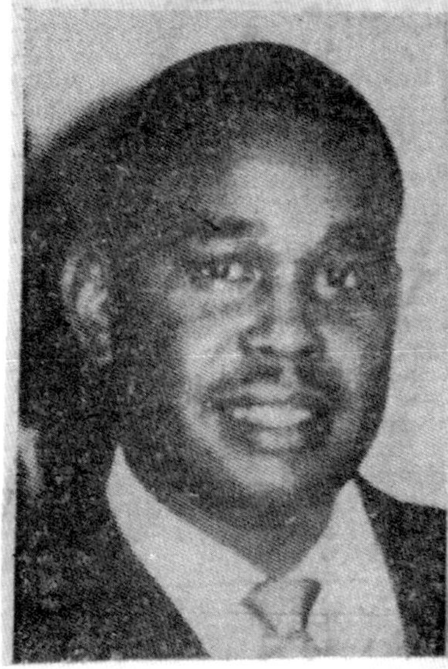

Gibson joined the AM&N College staff in 1959 as Director of Food Services and established during his first year a unique system, which brought him high praise from campus and state officials. He was promoted to Director of Student Union the following year.

Gibson is a native of Salem, New Jersey. He is a graduate of Tuskegee Institute, receiving his degree in commercial dietetics and institution management. Upon graduation in 1953, he worked on the staff at Tuskegee in the school of Commercial Dietetics for five years. In 1958, he entered graduate school at Michigan State University, East Lansing, Michigan, where he pursued the master's degree in the school of Hotel, Restaurant and Institution Management.

Gibson took an active part in campus and civic life during his tenure at AM&N. He served as sponsor of several student groups and just recently was elected president of the J. C. Corbin Laboratory School (AM&N College) PTA.

"Naturally, it is a difficult decision to make. Leaving a community which has given me so much cooperation and confidence is tough. However, I am now realizing a life-time dream to go into management of a fine restaurant. The opportunity is so great that I feel I cannot let it pass," Gibson said.

Moving into the new position with Mr. Gibson will be his wife, Mrs. Carolyn B. Gibson, formerly of Little Rock, Arkansas. Mrs. Gibson is at present Director of Testing Services in the Student Personnel area at AM&N College with a degree in sociology and has done further study at the University of Arkansas and Mich. State University in the area of Guidance Education.

The Gibsons are the parents of two daughters, Stephanie Yvonne, the elder, who is in the sixth grade at Corbin Laboratory School and

Birmingham World news article. *Courtesy of Birmingham Civil Rights Institute.*

Gaston was planning a trip to Hot Springs, Arkansas, for his "annual bath." The springs there were believed to be a fountain of youth. In preparation for the trip, he contacted Ed Ramsey, a dean at Tuskegee University, in hopes that the man could help put him in touch with Gibson.

After Ramsey's prodding, Gibson agreed to meet with Gaston, but reluctantly so. Again, Gaston offered him a job managing the motel. Again, Gibson refused. A move would be worth his while only if he could own the place, he told Gaston. But Gibson felt that wasn't an option since he did not have the money to purchase it.

"If you know anything about Mr. Gaston, he is a very, very, very aggressive individual," Gibson said. Gaston told him that he would work out an option-to-buy deal that would allow Gibson to gradually buy the place. Shortly thereafter, Ernest and his family were headed to Birmingham.

"Naturally, it is a difficult decision to make," Gibson told *Birmingham World*. "Leaving a community which has given me so much cooperation and confidence is tough. However, I am now realizing a lifetime dream to go into management of a fine restaurant. The opportunity is so great that I feel I cannot let it pass."

"At that time we had a one-year-old, Dorothy, and an eleven-year-old, Stephanie, but we knew that with our energy, we could handle it," said his wife, Carolyn, who was director of testing services in student personnel at Arkansas AM&N.

"I loved Pine Bluff; that's where I grew up," said Stephanie. "I was not excited about leaving."

But if they had had a crystal ball, they might have made a different choice.

"We knew how bad it was in Alabama, but we had no idea of what was going to happen in the pipeline," Carolyn said. "I think if we had, we may not have gone."

A First-Class Facility

The year 1963 kicked off with fanfare. On January 11, the outgoing Alabama governor, John Patterson, named Gaston to the board of directors at Tuskegee Institute, an honor. A week later, on January 18, incoming Alabama governor George Wallace gave his now famous inaugural speech touting, "Segregation now, segregation tomorrow, segregation forever."[77]

When the Gibsons arrived in Birmingham for their February 1, 1963 start day, right away they found the motel not up to their standards. "The place was somewhat run-down," Ernest said.

"Whoever had been the manager did not do a good job. Mr. Gaston realized that," Mrs. Gibson said. "It wasn't the first-class place he wanted it to be. The building was in bad repair; the restaurant was not up to our standards. We immediately said to Mr. Gaston that we needed to make some renovations."

Gibson requested that the place be totally remodeled from carpet to furniture, kitchen to rooms. Gaston agreed, and the restaurant closed right away. A.H. Smith Construction Company was hired to take the job. Stanley B. Echols, who was the architect for the motel when it opened, did the renovations. The total cost of it was $65,000. It helped that, by then, Gaston had a real estate investment company and a Citizens Federal Savings and Loan bank in his coffer, Gibson said.

As repairs were underway, Gaston told the local media that when the restaurant reopened, it would "compete favorably with any other in the city."[78]

Stephanie remembered those days well. "I remember being in the kitchen and watching the automated milkshake machine being put in and the bright, shiny modern kitchen," she said.

The renovations took about a month to complete. Carolyn said she and "Ernie" spent their February 22 wedding anniversary among the construction in the coffee shop.

At the same time, the Gibsons were busy staffing a team of workers who would be able to provide service to their liking. Several people began to quit, Gibson said, because they did not want to subscribe to his new, stricter program. Gibson and his wife even created a makeshift school to train workers to be high-quality motel maids, kitchen staff, etc. They taught classes on how to wait tables and how to cook. There were weekly classes that featured lectures from experts in the field of service.

Gibson told the local media that "the personnel will be trained to fit into the A.G. Gaston Restaurant system and oriented into high standards." He hired people away from the white hotels and motels, including employing the head housekeeper from the Holiday Inn from over the mountain.

"We changed out all of the maids, equipment, individuals in key appointments. Some stayed because they adhered to the program," he said. "We cleaned up the situation."

The dining room service staff included Arzell Skipwith, Catherine Lenoir, Jerushia Thornton, Pearl Tarver, Bertha Quinn, Ida T. Johnson, Stephanie Gibson, Gladys Hildreth, Maxcine Robinson, Catherine Smith, Iola

World 2-23-1963

A. G. Gaston Restaurant Under New Management

The A G Gaston Restaurant, now under management o Ernest F. Gibson, is scheduled to re-open March 1 with new services, improved facilities and fresh renovations.

The restaurant has been closed for repairs since Feb. 1. Mr. Gibson indicated that improvements have been made at a cost of approximately $65,000. He added that the downtown facility when re-opened for dining will compare favorably with any other in the city.

Under the improvements there will be the Gastonian Room which will have two daily dining periods — 10 P M to 2 P. M and 5 P M to 12 P. M.

There will be wall to wall carpeting in the Gastonian Room. There will be a more formal setting for dining. The atmosphere will be gracious and the tone congenial. The facility will accommodate 150 persons and will be available for parties and banquets. Carolyn Gibson will be the hostess.

The Coffee Shop will operate from 7 A M. through 12 P M. Curb service and take -out service. The Coffee Shop will operate a thrift section. This will include a counter where customers will be able to get fast service.

Mr. Gibson said that in the Gastonian Room there will be introduced party time and banquet time Catering service on and off premises will be provided. He added that the Louis Richar Hall Auditorium (A. G Gaston Building) will serve as an outlet for banquets and related activities.

To insure top - quality service Mr. Gibson announced that he is conducting a "School for Waitresses" and a "School for Cooks." He added that the personnel will be trained to fit into the A. G. Gaston Restaurant system and oriented into high standards.

Additionally he sai that renovated A G Gaston Restaurant will have a foyer.

"The target date for re-opening," Mr. Gibson reminded, "is Friday, Mar. 1.

Above: *Birmingham World* news article. *Courtesy of Birmingham Civil Rights Institute.*

Below: *Birmingham World* advertisement. *Courtesy of Birmingham Civil Rights Institute.*

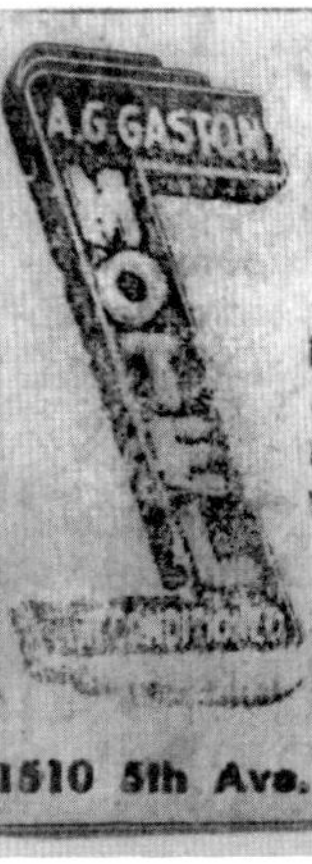

A. G. GASTON'S

DRIVE-IN RESTAURANT

OPENS TWENTY HOURS DAILY

7:00 A.M. – 3:00 A.M.

PRIVATE DINING ROOM — CATERING TO PARTIES AND BANQUETS AMPLE PARKING FACILITIES

Specializing in . . Sea Foods
'Gaston's - Special" Steak
Fresh – Jumbo Shrimps
Three Delicious Meals Daily

For Reservations Dial AL 2-9393

1510 5th Ave. W 4-16-60 Birmingham, Ala.

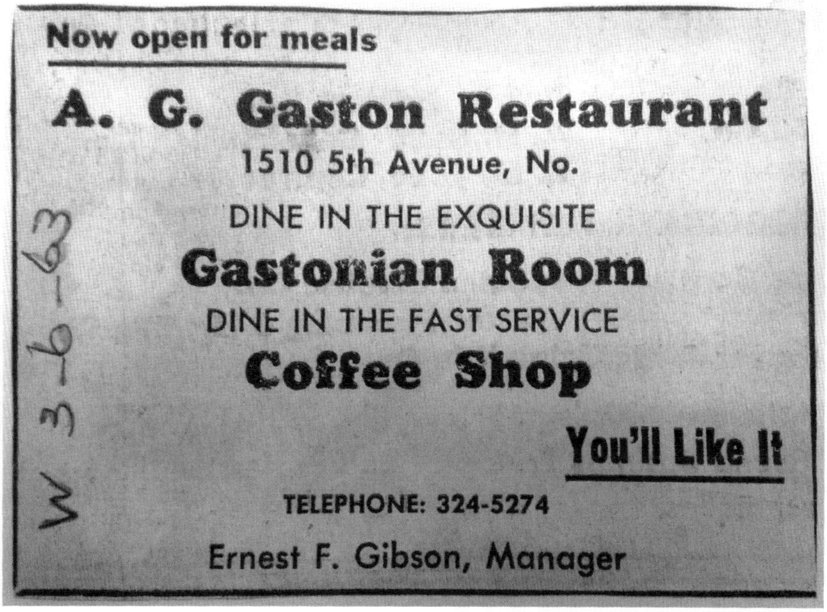

Birmingham World advertisement. *Courtesy of Birmingham Civil Rights Institute.*

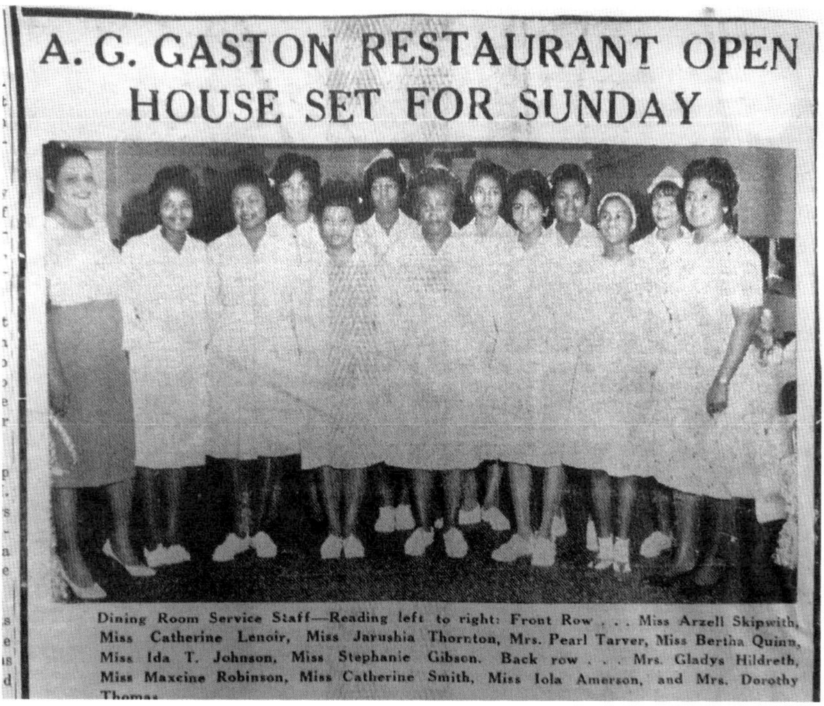

A. G. GASTON RESTAURANT OPEN HOUSE SET FOR SUNDAY

Dining Room Service Staff—Reading left to right: Front Row . . . Miss Arzell Skipwith, Miss Catherine Lenoir, Miss Jarushia Thornton, Mrs. Pearl Tarver, Miss Bertha Quinn, Miss Ida T. Johnson, Miss Stephanie Gibson. Back row . . . Mrs. Gladys Hildreth, Miss Maxcine Robinson, Miss Catherine Smith, Miss Iola Amerson, and Mrs. Dorothy Thomas.

Birmingham World news article. *Courtesy of Birmingham Civil Rights Institute.*

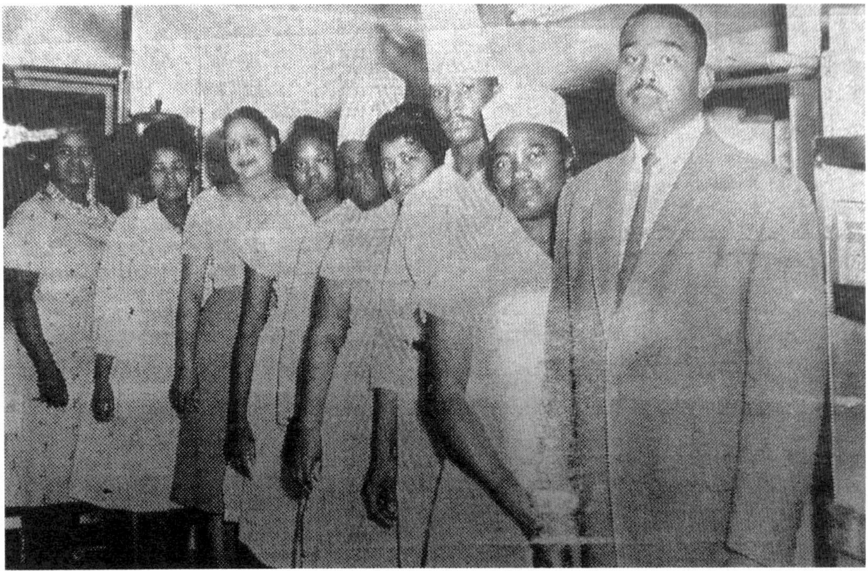

Birmingham World news article. *Courtesy of Birmingham Civil Rights Institute.*

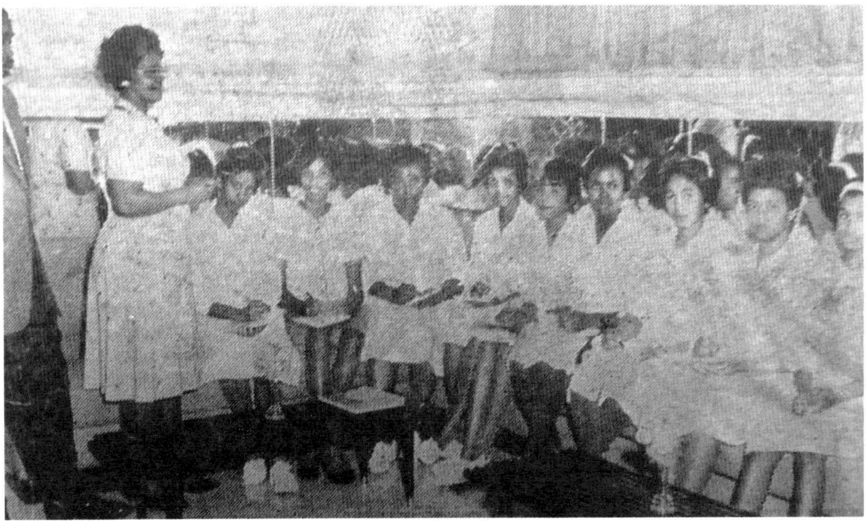

Birmingham World news article. *Courtesy of Birmingham Civil Rights Institute.*

Amerson and Dorothy Thomas. The kitchen staff was made up of Adell Bonham, Eugene Fikes, Miss Bobbie, J. Ferguson, Jesse Shannon, Miss Augusta and Miss Atkins.

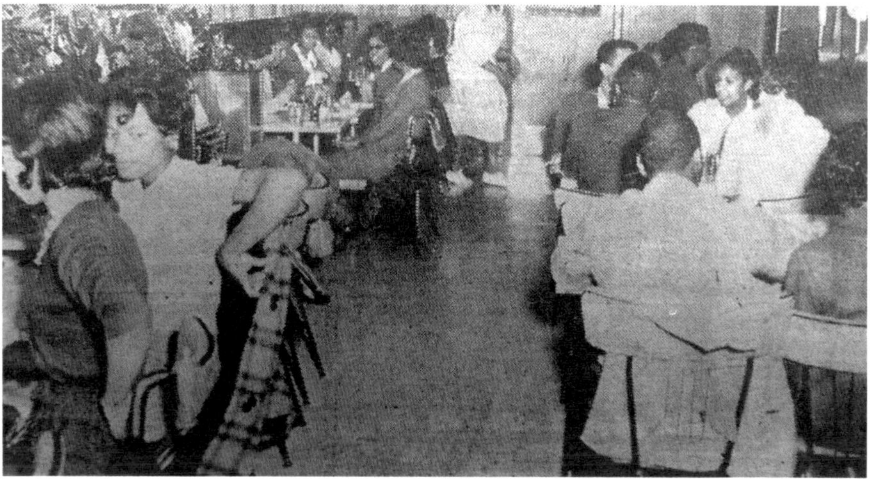

Birmingham World news article. *Courtesy of Birmingham Civil Rights Institute.*

"They were excited about the work they were doing and opening up the new A.G. Gaston Motel," Ernest said. "We had a good spirited corps of employees."

They added all new furniture, paintings on the walls and electric fixtures. They put in a new coffee shop and a formal dining room. Ernest changed the name of the lounge to the Gastonian Room.

The restaurant reopened on Friday, March 1, with what *Birmingham World* called "new services, improved facilities, and a revitalized character." The Gibsons were front and center. Ernest was the manager, his wife was the official hostess and Stephanie served as the cashier and worked the switchboard after school and on the weekends. "At that point, my father was supposed to ultimately own that motel, so we considered that our family business," Stephanie said.

"The results of these classes are already being reflected in greatly improved table service, and quality in dispatch in preparation and serving of food," *Birmingham World* noted.

The 150-person-capacity restaurant featured two sets of dining hours, from 10:00 a.m. to 2:00 p.m. and 5:00 p.m. to midnight. The coffee shop, which was decked with walnut paneling, featured hours from 7:00 a.m. to 12:00 p.m. It also featured curb and takeout service and boasted fast service. "We tried to make it appropriate for morning 'til night," Carolyn said.

"They got rid of the malt shop and added a bar," Washington remembers. "I was of age at the time, and it suited me just fine."

The Gastonian Room featured a plate-glass divider that separated it from the coffee shop. The "luxurious foyer created by gold metal dividers, lends itself to more formality and versatility in service to large as well as

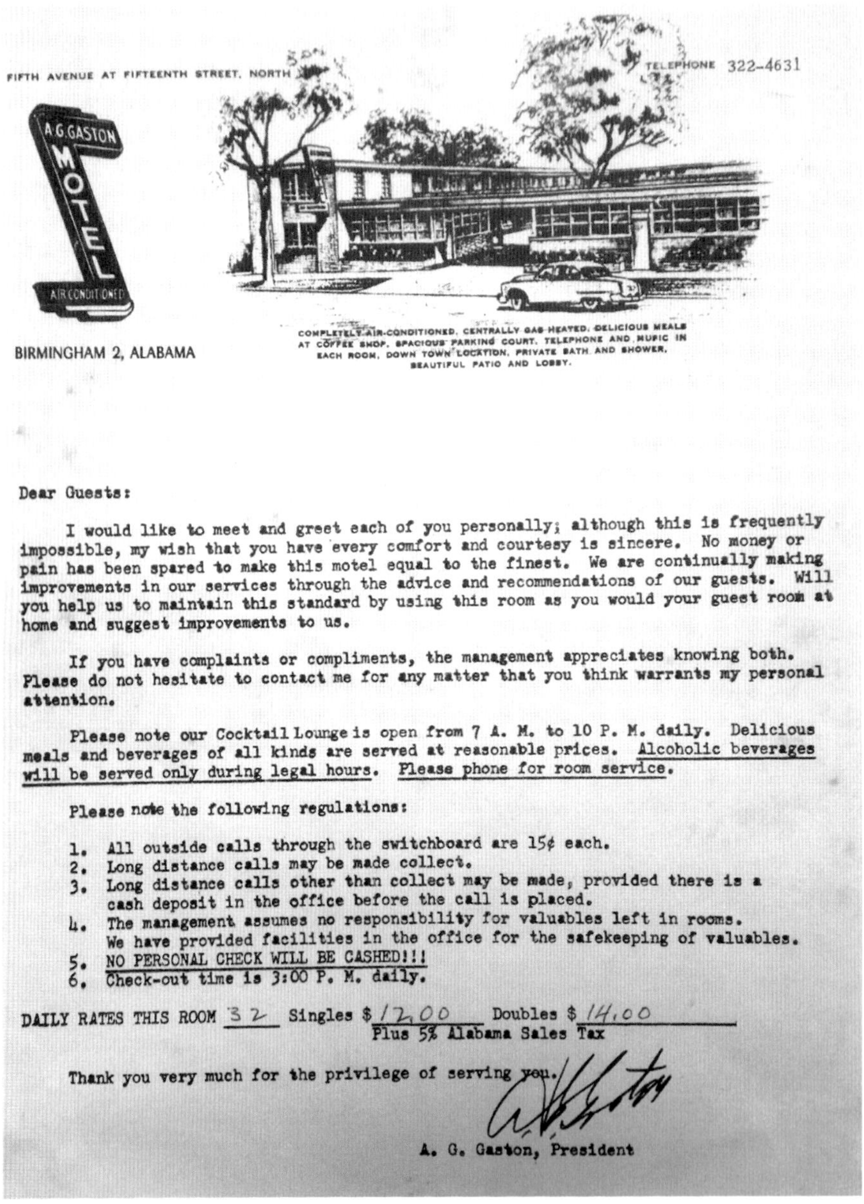

FIFTH AVENUE AT FIFTEENTH STREET, NORTH

TELEPHONE 322-4631

A.G. GASTON MOTEL AIR CONDITIONED

BIRMINGHAM 2, ALABAMA

COMPLETELY AIR-CONDITIONED, CENTRALLY GAS HEATED, DELICIOUS MEALS AT COFFEE SHOP, SPACIOUS PARKING COURT, TELEPHONE AND MUSIC IN EACH ROOM, DOWN TOWN LOCATION, PRIVATE BATH AND SHOWER, BEAUTIFUL PATIO AND LOBBY.

Dear Guests:

I would like to meet and greet each of you personally; although this is frequently impossible, my wish that you have every comfort and courtesy is sincere. No money or pain has been spared to make this motel equal to the finest. We are continually making improvements in our services through the advice and recommendations of our guests. Will you help us to maintain this standard by using this room as you would your guest room at home and suggest improvements to us.

If you have complaints or compliments, the management appreciates knowing both. Please do not hesitate to contact me for any matter that you think warrants my personal attention.

Please note our Cocktail Lounge is open from 7 A. M. to 10 P. M. daily. Delicious meals and beverages of all kinds are served at reasonable prices. Alcoholic beverages will be served only during legal hours. Please phone for room service.

Please note the following regulations:

1. All outside calls through the switchboard are 15¢ each.
2. Long distance calls may be made collect.
3. Long distance calls other than collect may be made, provided there is a cash deposit in the office before the call is placed.
4. The management assumes no responsibility for valuables left in rooms. We have provided facilities in the office for the safekeeping of valuables.
5. NO PERSONAL CHECK WILL BE CASHED!!!
6. Check-out time is 3:00 P. M. daily.

DAILY RATES THIS ROOM 32 Singles $12.00 Doubles $14.00
Plus 5% Alabama Sales Tax

Thank you very much for the privilege of serving you.

A. G. Gaston, President

The Gaston Motel check-in letter. *Courtesy of the Birmingham Civil Rights Institute.*

small parties and banquets." The room also had mural paintings, vinyl wall coverings and modern abstract wall mounts.

There was wall-to-wall carpeting and indirect lighting and suspended light fixtures. There were metal and leather "vari-colored" Herman Miller chairs, which are "used in the finest clubs," according to *Birmingham World.*

"No pains or expense was spared in revitalizing these dining areas," the writer noted.

The official open house was on Sunday, March 24, at 2:00 p.m. *Birmingham World* featured ads from the list of proud vendors that participated in the renovation: the National Cash Register Co., D. Lee and Sons Grocery Co., City Paper Company, Barber's Pure Milk and Ice Cream Company, Royal Cup Coffee, Empire Seafood Co. Inc., Means Company, Inc., Plumbing & Heating Contractors, Rutland Baking Co., Arrow-Smith Heating & Air Conditioning, J.A. Blackmon Co., Independent Fish Company Inc., Howard Johnson Electric Company and New Ideal Department Store.

The food was traditional restaurant cuisine with elegant offerings such as shrimp and lobster but also with an emphasis on African American culture. It also had featured menus at certain times during the year to bring in different holidays.

"We were a continental concept of food offerings," Ernest said. "If you are going to open a restaurant, you have to cater to the local clientele."

Every aspect of the Gaston Motel experience was thought about. When guests checked in, they received a letter from Gaston:

> *Dear Guests,*
>
> *I would like to meet and greet each of you personally; although this is frequently impossible, my wish that you have every comfort and courtesy is sincere. No money or pain has been spared to make this motel equal to the finest. We are continually making improvements in our services through the advice and recommendations of our guests. Will you help us to maintain this standard by using the room as you would your guest room at home and suggest improvements to us.*
>
> *If you have complaints or compliments, the management appreciates knowing both. Please do not hesitate to contact me for any matter that you think warrants my personal attention.*
>
> *Please note our Cocktail lounge is open from 7 a.m. to 10 p.m. daily. Delicious meals and beverages of all kinds are served at reasonable prices. Alcoholic beverages will be served only during legal hours. Please phone for room service.*

Please note the following regulations:

1. All outside calls through switchboard are 15 cents each.
2. Long distance calls may be made collect.
3. Long distance calls other than collect may be made, provided there is a cash deposit in the office before the call is placed.
4. The management assumes no responsibility for valuables left in rooms. We have provided facilities in our office for the safekeeping of valuables.
5. NO PERSONAL CHECK WILL BE CASHED.
6. Check-out time is 3:00 p.m. daily.

DAILY RATES THIS ROOM 32 Singles $12.00 Doubles $14.00
Plus 5% Alabama Sales Tax
Thank you very much for the privilege of serving you.

A.G. Gaston, President

Across the street from the motel, the Gaston Building had many offices, a large auditorium and business school. Customers were ripe, Gibson said. "We were in a perfect spot," he said. "It ended up being a meeting place where most people came every day or every night."

"Angela Davis's father owned a print shop around the corner," Gibson said of the political activist's dad. "He came in every day to have lunch. All the professionals came: the pharmacists, lawyers, etc. all flocked there."

The Gibsons opened a catering business that made itself available for events at L.R. Hall Auditorium, which had soirées with two to five hundred persons. Gibson was a member of Alpha Phi Alpha Fraternity, Inc. and his wife a member of Delta Sigma Theta Sorority, Inc. This positioned them with the contacts to host many black sorority and fraternity functions, as well as all the social clubs for adults and youngsters, like Jack and Jill and Tot and Teens, he said.

"We had a thriving business…for a while."

According to an article by Mayo Toal Forniss in *Birmingham World*, the Birmingham Chapter of Links hosted the 1963 Southern Area Links gathering on March 15–17. This national organization was made of distinguished women from across the country who were committed to volunteer service. On that Friday night, the women had a "lavish" reception at L.R. Hall, where "gorgeously attired ladies" met Mr. and Mrs. Birmingham, according to the article.

During a Saturday morning business session, Gaston gave greetings. His wife, Minnie, was among the participants. She was the national treasurer for the organization. Later that day, the Gastonian Room was the scene for a candlelit banquet. Miles College president Pitts was the guest speaker. Edythe Jones presided. Dean Cohen Simpson of Talladega College blessed the food. Oralee Barranco Mitchell of the New Orleans chapter was named Woman of the Year. Jessie Vick, president of the Fayetteville, North Carolina chapter, accepted the award for Outstanding Chapter Project. The national officers and regional director each received orchids.

On Sunday morning, the ladies gathered again at the Gastonian Room for a breakfast party and goodbyes. Link Vara Hinton presided. "Sad goodbyes were voiced as parting time came," the reporter wrote.

Samuetta Drew remembers that her parents went to the Gaston for dinner every Sunday after church. It was inspiring to see the name of a black man on the outside of a building and know that inside there was a first-class facility, she said.

"It was the place to go for fine dining," she said, recalling the soft music, white tablecloths and waiters who were dressed to impress. "You didn't order from the counter," Drew remarked. "You sat down."

She remembers the nice, tall printed menus with black backs and "A.G. Gaston" embossed on them in gold. There was a divider painted with gold circles, "like in the movies," she said.

The menu was luxurious for the times, she said: seafood, steaks, pork and chicken.

"It was a place we could go and be treated with dignity," she said. "It was a place you could go and feel proud. You did not have to be a kid in the window of a candy shop looking in. You could go inside and partake."

Dale Long's parents treated him and his friends to dinner at Gaston's in honor of their graduation. This was their first experience eating at a restaurant. "It was the first time I ever ate shrimp," Long said. "Black kids didn't have that experience," he said. His brother ate the shrimp, too, the tails and all.

There were many middle-class blacks who wanted to have an experience. "You knew that lifestyle was available," Drew said. "It gave you a sense of who you are: not a second-class citizen, although everything around you was saying that," she said. "It showed you that if you wanted to own something, you could."

Her mother was a member of Club Excelsior's for teachers, and every Saturday after Christmas, they held their New Year's Eve brunch there. It was a tradition. Everyone wore after-five attire. Drew said she could not wait to get older so that she could be among the group.

Pretty soon, the Gibsons began to realize that they were uniquely positioned not just to host social affairs but also to be part of the civil rights movement—whether they wanted to or not.

Over in Collegeville, Shuttlesworth was working tirelessly. He sent a petition to Commissioner Art Hanes requesting the desegregation of public facilities. Hanes, ever resistant, sent him a letter saying that the petition had been trashed.

Shuttlesworth needed King's help again. He sent word to him: "If you come to Birmingham, you will not only gain prestige, but really shake the country. If you win in Birmingham, as Birmingham goes, so goes the nation."[79]

King and his group of activists and strategists heard his cry and made plans to come.

"On April 3—having held off as long as was necessary—Martin and I flew to Birmingham to begin our most ambitious campaign," Reverend Ralph Abernathy wrote in *And the Walls Came Tumbling Down*.[80] The SCLC and Shuttlesworth's ACMHR joined for a campaign of sit-ins at local lunch counters.[81]

Together, they had a list of demands:

> *The desegregation of lunch counters, restrooms, fitting rooms and drinking fountains in variety and department stores.*
>
> *The upgrading and hiring of Negroes on a nondiscriminatory basis throughout the business and industrial community of Birmingham.*
>
> *The dropping of all charges against jailed demonstrators.*
>
> *The creation of a biracial committee to work out a timetable for desegregation in other areas of Birmingham life.*[82]

"The Gaston Motel was Birmingham's only acceptable black inn, the place where black business and professional people stayed when they visited the city," Abernathy wrote.[83] King entered the motel and approached Gibson about taking over the place.

"Martin came in with a group—Wyatt Tee Walker, Andy Young, Abernathy and Shuttlesworth," Gibson remembered. "They all came in and met with me in reference to the fact that they would like to take over all of the rooms and did I have any problem with it.

"I said that I did not, but I could not give them all of the rooms. I am a member of the motel association, and I have to have a portion of the facilities available. They went along with it. Immediately, Dr. King took over the main suite."

It was fate, the men thought. "Dr. King was so pleased that I was at the motel," said Gibson. King said it was meant to be, that "God sent you here," Gibson remembered.

Gibson's friendship with King was born back in Gibson's Tuskegee University days. They met in Tuskegee right after King got his doctorate in Boston and was taking over the Dexter Avenue Baptist Church in Montgomery. At the time, Gibson was active with the Tuskegee Civic Association, an organization that was very involved in civil rights in Macon County. Gibson and the group regularly fought for the right to vote, to get public accommodations and to "get things that we as citizens should have bestowed upon us."

Senator Sam Engelhardt of Macon County was a state legislator at the time and did not like that movement, Gibson said. "He tried to gerrymander us out of Macon County," Gibson remembered. "We fought him as the civic organization. We took it to the Supreme Court and won."

When King, who was just miles up the road in Montgomery, heard about the courageous group, he and fellow minister Ralph Abernathy came to Tuskegee to study the movement. Gibson was impressed with young King, he said. "He was so dynamic and articulate," Gibson said. "Then he was an Alpha."

Gibson, who was an Episcopalian, decided instead to attend King's Baptist church. The two became friends, he said. Gibson supported King in Montgomery during the bus boycott.

"When I accepted the position to buy the motel, I did not accept on the premise that Martin would come in with the movement," Gibson said. Even though it has been said that the motel was retrofitted for the movement, that is not true, according to Gibson. "Gaston didn't want the movement there at all," he said. "Mr. Gaston was not in favor of Dr. King coming to Birmingham."

And he wasn't alone. Many people saw King and the others as outsiders coming to agitate an already sensitive situation. There was a line drawn in the sand between King and Shuttlesworth supporters versus Gaston's. According to historian Glenn Eskew, Emory O. Jackson, the editor of *Birmingham World*, the black weekly newspaper, supported Gaston's side. "He said little about Shuttlesworth and King as attested by the lack of coverage in the *World*," Eskew wrote.[31]

Still, King and his group settled into the motel because there was a mission at hand. The men came and set up what would be called Project C, which stood for "confrontation." Shuttlesworth issued the Birmingham Manifesto, which explained how past attempts to bring about change had been met with resistance and now civil disobedience and direct action would be justified.

He and the men of SCLC planned a series of direct nonviolent action, which included sit-ins, marches and kneel-ins at area lunch counters, churches and libraries. They knew Bull Connor, a staunch segregationist, and his cronies were reactionary and were banking on their behavior to shame them before a national audience. Also, they knew that boycotting retailers that supported segregation would hit them where it hurts: their pockets. Easter was around the corner and was one of the largest shopping seasons. Movement supporters were encouraged not to patronize these businesses.

Those plans were drawn up in room 30 at the Gaston Motel, King and the others said. Abernathy remembered that the suite he and King shared was a one-bedroom with two double beds and a sitting room with chairs, a table and a desk.

"It was in that sitting room that most of the strategy was hatched during the campaign," Abernathy wrote.[85]

Demonstrators launched sit-ins at area restaurants and were arrested. Shuttlesworth and several protesters led a march to city hall and were promptly put in jail. Supporters of King and the Birmingham movement began to flood into town to link arms with the men. Famous jazz musician Al Hibbler joined the protesters and was arrested though later released.

Chapter 6

ENOUGH IS ENOUGH

The Gaston was the nucleus of the civil rights movement.
—Dale Long, who grew up playing around the motel

Although the movement was moving forward, the widespread support of locals was not there. The SCLC wanted the jails of Birmingham to be overflowing with protestors, but that wasn't happening.

Shelley Stewart remembered that King, Walker and Shuttlesworth didn't wait for people to show up. While at his record store, Shelley's Record Mart on 1607 Fifth Avenue North, Stewart remembered that King and others came in and bemoaned how difficult it was to get marchers. "Hey, Shelley, I sure need these people to get fired up and march," King told Stewart. "They won't come to the meeting."

But King wasn't about to let dust gather around his feet. He said, "I am going down to the poolroom."

"That's right, the *preacher*," Stewart recalled. King and the men headed into the Fourth Avenue District, where there were countless bars, including a shoeshine place where, as quiet as it was kept, you could get whiskey in the back. King went downstairs to the poolroom in the Masonic Temple.

"An hour later, I am turning in front of my store at Seventeenth Street and Fifth Avenue North. I see Martin and about forty or fifty men following him. They were saying, 'Freedom! Freedom!' I said, 'What in the world?'"

Stewart described the sight of King and Wyatt walking in step with winos and "some guys I knew from around the way."

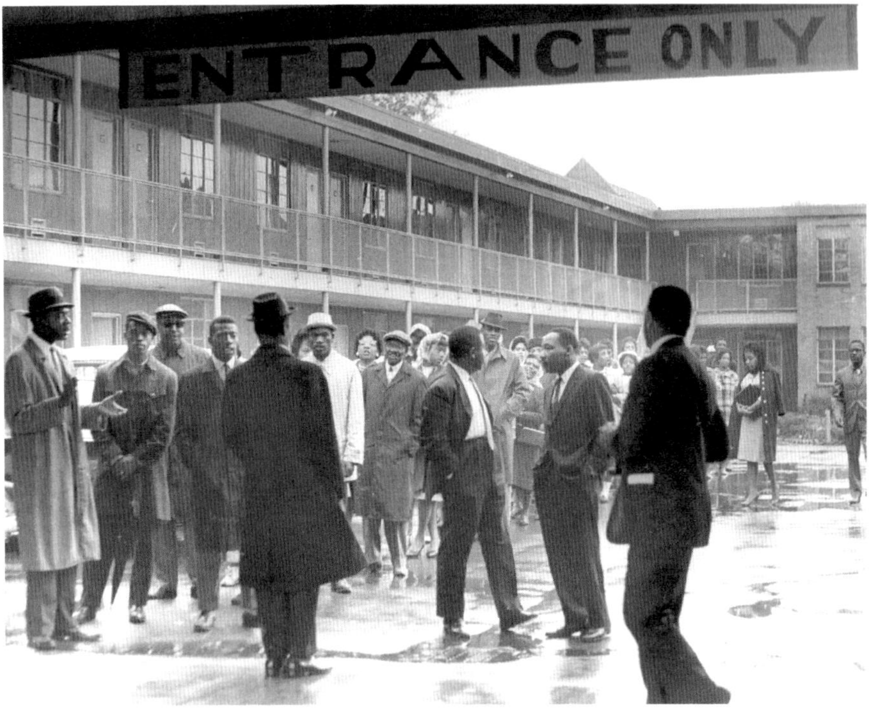

Dr. King stands in the Gaston Motel courtyard. *Courtesy of Birmingham Public Library.*

"What Martin did, he went to the poolroom, restaurant, the bar and down to Rat Killer's. Everywhere he stopped, he told folks, 'I need you to stand up for freedom and join me,'" Stewart remembered.

King and the group went to the courtyard of the Gaston Motel. King climbed up the stairs and faced the men so that the group could see him. "Can y'all get double what we have?" he asked them.

"He took winos and guys who were on the block. They were there when others wouldn't come," Stewart recalled. "That's what it was all about. In that parking lot, that inspired me to do something that came after that."

It inspired Stewart to do his part, to use the airways to encourage people to stand up for freedom.

But the tensions between King's group and those who felt he was out of line for stirring up trouble had grown. Religious leaders, political influencers and the like were speaking out against King, describing him as an outsider. Many felt the segregation issue should be handled in the courts and that he was stirring up people. They thought a protest on Easter Sunday was out of line.

On April 8, King met with local black leaders at the Gaston Building so that he could make an appeal and hopefully gather support for his planned protest. It turned out to be a showdown instead. Later that night, in response, Abernathy gave a biting sermon at First Baptist Church of Ensley.[36] The *Cleveland Call and Post* wrote that he "scathingly assailed the black 'bourgeoisie' to the howling delight of the rafter-packed audience."

"Talk to your doctor, your lawyer, your insurance man and withdraw your trade from him if he is not with the movement," Abernathy told them.

The next day, April 9, Gaston released a statement to *Birmingham World* that sent movement people through the roof:

> *I regret the absence of continued communication between the white and Negro leadership in our city and the inability of the white merchants and white power structure of community to influence the City Fathers to establish an official line of communication between the races in our city.*
>
> *This condition, along with the many unsolved bombings and other incidents causing unfavorable publicity for Birmingham has made this city a very attractive target for the present unhappy situation in which we now find ourselves.*
>
> *There is no doubt in my mind or in the minds of any of us, concerning the aspirations of the Negro citizens in this community and throughout the country. We want freedom and justice; and we want to be able to live and work with dignity in all endeavors where we are qualified. We also want the privilege of access to those facilities that will make an individual qualified. We also want to contribute our share for the progress of our community I believe we have capable and intelligent leadership among the colored people in the community, competent and able to work toward bringing the hopes, dreams and aspirations of the Negro citizens to reality.*
>
> *The problem that Birmingham now faces were faced by other great Southern cities and, to the credit of these great cities, which lie within a short distance of us, the local leaders of their communities got their minds, talents and energies together and solved their respective problems.*
>
> *Today, Birmingham now stands on the threshold of transition to greatness. The sails have been set for the City and it is now incumbent on the leadership of this community to chart its destiny.*
>
> *I therefore call upon all the citizens of Birmingham to work harmoniously and together in a spirit of brotherly love to solve the problems of our city, giving due recognition to the local colored leadership among us.*
>
> *A.G. Gaston, Sr.*

This was seen by King as a slight to him and the other non-locals. Shuttlesworth was fuming. He had moved to Cincinnati, Ohio, in 1961 but was still leading the Birmingham movement. The "locals" remark seemed like an attack. He accused Gaston of being "a Super Uncle Tom" and claimed that he charged too much for his rooms at the motel.[87]

People were considering protesting Gaston and his businesses, but Ed Gardner, a local minister and Gaston advocate, warned that if the group proceeded, he and his group of ministers would run them out of town.

Soon afterward, Shuttlesworth retracted his statement and apologized.

In order to bring the groups together, King set up an advisory committee of twenty-five men and women who would meet daily in the Gaston Motel to be briefed on the day's events.

On April 10, Bull Connor got an injunction that made it illegal for protestors to march. It also raised the bail amount to four times its original, from $300 to $1,200. Connor vowed, "You can rest assured that I will fill the jail full of any persons violating the law as long as I'm at city hall."

Now the movement was at a crossroads. Would it proceed with planned protests and break the law? Also, raising the bail amount meant protestors needed more money. Their biggest fundraiser, King, didn't need to be arrested. He needed to raise more funds. But the people who had volunteered to go to jail were looking for their leader to follow them there.

To add to that, on April 12, which was Good Friday, eight clergy in Birmingham posted a statement in the *Birmingham News* noting that the march was "unwise and untimely."[88] They urged "our Negro community to withdraw support from these demonstrators, and to unite locally and work peacefully for a better Birmingham." The men included the Right Reverend C.J. Carpenter, Episcopal bishop of Alabama; Reverend Joseph A. Durrick, auxiliary Roman Catholic bishop; and Rabbi Hilton Grafman of Temple Emanuel.[89]

> *From "A Group of Clergymen" published in the* Birmingham News
> *We clergymen are among those who, in January, issued "an Appeal for Law and Order and Common Sense," in dealing with racial problems in Alabama. We expressed understanding that honest convictions in racial matters could properly be pursued in the courts, but urged that decisions of those courts should in the meantime be peacefully obeyed.*
>
> *...We are now confronted by a series of demonstrations by some of our Negro citizens, directed and led in part by outsiders. We recognize the natural impatience of people who feel that their hopes are slow*

> *in being realized. But we are convinced that these demonstrations are unwise and untimely.*
>
> *...Just as we formerly pointed out that "hatred and violence have no sanction in our religious and political traditions," we also point out that such actions as incite to hatred and violence, however technically peaceful those actions may be, have not contributed to the resolution of our local problems. We do not believe that these days of new hope are days when extreme measures are justified in Birmingham.*
>
> *...We further strongly urge our own Negro community to withdraw support from these demonstrations, and to unite locally in working peacefully for a better Birmingham. When rights are consistently denied, a cause should be pressed in the courts and in negotiations among local leaders, and not in the streets. We appeal to both our white and Negro citizenry to observe the principles of law and order and common sense.*[90]

"Martin was particularly disturbed when he read it, shaking his head and wondering how religious leaders could encourage the kind of attitude that had created a city where bombing of black houses and churches had become almost a common occurrence," Abernathy wrote. "He brooded about the statement long after he should have dismissed it from his mind."

As a result, shortly after that, King's own advisory committee also asked him not to march. "They cited the need to obey the law and their own belief that things might get out of hand, that perhaps we needed a cooling off period; that it would be improper to violate the sanctity of the Easter season by acts of disobedience that might provoke violence."[91]

All twenty-five of them met in the Gaston suite to discuss the different arguments. "So we sat there in the motel suite and for a while allowed them to lecture us on the virtues of prudence and compromise," Abernathy wrote.[92]

At the same time, a crowd was gathering in Sixteenth Street Baptist Church, where King's staff was getting them ready, "taking away their guns, knives and razors and telling them that they must learn to cover their heads and never strike out, even when attacked."[93] King remembers having to decide on that Good Friday whether to walk outside the motel to march and surely be arrested.

"No one knew what to say, for no one knew what to do," King wrote. "I was alone in that crowded room."[94]

King dismissed himself, went to the back of the suite and stood at the center of the floor, he said.

"I think I was standing at the center of all that my life had brought me to be," King wrote. "I thought of the Birmingham Negro community, waiting.

Then my mind leaped beyond the Gaston Motel, past city lines and state lines, and I thought of the twenty million black people who dreamed that someday they might be able to cross the Red Sea of injustice and find their way to the Promised Land of integration and freedom. There was no more room for doubt."[95]

He changed into "work" clothes and went back to the crowd waiting.

"I don't know what will happen; I don't know where the money will come from. But I have to make a faith act," he told them.

King walked up to Abernathy and told him that he was going to march. He said that his father could be there for his Atlanta congregation on Easter, but since Abernathy had no one to cover his church service on that day, he should go back to Atlanta.

"Then he reached out and embraced me," Abernathy wrote.[96] "I knew what he was thinking: He might either be arrested and jailed for months or else be killed, given the pent-up emotions about to be loosed.

"He was giving me a way out," Abernathy continued. "But on this Good Friday, I wasn't about to be Peter."[97]

Abernathy declared that he would be joining King.

King linked arms with the others, and right there in the room, they sang in unison "We Shall Overcome."

Later that day, King and Abernathy were arrested. They were put in separate jail cells, and for the first twenty-four hours, King was put in solitary confinement and not allowed any communication. "No one was permitted to visit me, not even my lawyers," King wrote. "Those were the longest, most frustrating and bewildering hours I have lived."[98]

King worried about his fellow marchers and his wife, Coretta, who had just given birth to their youngest child, Bernice. He didn't know what his arrest was doing to the morale of the people.

He had many questions.

"You will never know the meaning of utter darkness until you have lain in such a dungeon, knowing that sunlight is streaming overhead and seeing only darkness below,"[99] King wrote.

President John F. Kennedy was alerted of King's arrest, and he moved mountains to arrange for the minister's wife to call him. Also, King's attorneys, Arthur Shores and Orzell Billingsley, received permission to visit him. Not long after that, his friend and lawyer Clarence Jones from New York came for a visit. He told King that actor/singer Harry Belafonte had raised $50,000 for the bail money and had said, "Whatever else you need, he will raise it."

Those words "lifted a thousand pounds from my heart," King wrote.

April 14, Easter Sunday, arrived, and kneel-ins took place at white churches across the city.

While in jail, King penned a response to the clergy who had written to him earlier. He started writing it in the margins of a newspaper, then on scraps of paper and finally in a notebook he was able to attain. Wyatt got the letter and pieced it together in the Gaston Motel.[100] Here is part of what he wrote on April 16:

> *My Dear Fellow Clergymen:*
>
> *While confined here in the Birmingham city jail, I came across your recent statement calling my present activities "unwise and untimely." Seldom do I pause to answer criticism of my work and ideas...But since I feel that you are men of genuine good will and that your criticisms are sincerely set forth, I want to try to answer your statement in what I hope will be patient and reasonable terms.*
>
> *...I am in Birmingham because injustice is here...I cannot sit idly by in Atlanta and not be concerned about what happens in Birmingham. Injustice anywhere is a threat to justice everywhere. We are caught in an inescapable network of mutuality, tied in a single garment of destiny. Whatever affects one directly, affects all indirectly. Never again can we afford to live with the narrow, provincial "outside agitator" idea. Anyone who lives inside the United States can never be considered an outsider anywhere within its bounds.*
>
> *...We know through painful experience that freedom is never voluntarily given by the oppressor; it must be demanded by the oppressed.*
>
> *...Perhaps it is easy for those who have never felt the stinging darts of segregation to say, "Wait." But when you have seen vicious mobs lynch your mothers and fathers at will and drown your sisters and brothers at whim; when you have seen hate filled policemen curse, kick and even kill your black brothers and sisters; when you see the vast majority of your twenty million Negro brothers smothering in an airtight cage of poverty in the midst of an affluent society; when you suddenly find your tongue twisted and your speech stammering as you seek to explain to your six year old daughter why she can't go to the public amusement park that has just been advertised on television, and see tears welling up in her eyes when she is told that Funtown is closed to colored children, and see ominous clouds of inferiority beginning to form in her little mental sky, and see her beginning to distort her personality by developing an unconscious bitterness toward white*

people; when you have to concoct an answer for a five year old son who is asking: "Daddy, why do white people treat colored people so mean?"; when you take a cross country drive and find it necessary to sleep night after night in the uncomfortable corners of your automobile because no motel will accept you; when you are humiliated day in and day out by nagging signs reading "white" and "colored"; when your first name becomes "nigger," your middle name becomes "boy" (however old you are) and your last name becomes "John," and your wife and mother are never given the respected title "Mrs."; when you are harried by day and haunted by night by the fact that you are a Negro, living constantly at tiptoe stance, never quite knowing what to expect next, and are plagued with inner fears and outer resentments; when you are forever fighting a degenerating sense of "nobodiness"—then you will understand why we find it difficult to wait.[101]

Chapter 7

AND A CHILD WILL LEAD THEM

The longer King was in jail, the more the attention toward the movement's efforts grew. But in an unsolicited and controversial move, Gaston paid the bail for King and Abernathy's release. Gaston had always put up his money to help bail out protesters. In all, he had spent $160,000 of his money getting various demonstrators out of jail.[102] But the timing of this was not well received by some.

Andrew Young saw red. Gaston's intentions for bailing out the men, Young felt, were "to persuade [King] to stop the demonstration and leave Birmingham."[103]

Gaston was "an Uncle Tom in the best sense," he wrote.[104] "He milked the system of segregation for millions of dollars." Young suggested that Gaston "couldn't sustain the enterprises without cooperation from white establishments: supplies could delay his deliveries; government inspections could find violations of state codes in his service businesses; local banks could refuse to honor his credit."[105]

"Gaston was a master at survival; he made money on segregation, and he made money during the movement—not one of us ever stayed a night free in Gaston's Motel."

But King wasn't angry. He accepted the bail and felt his release would allow him to be on-site to give strategy and solidarity. His release was the needed shot in the arm for his supporters, he felt.

On April 25, NAACP executive secretary Roy Wilkins spoke at Sixteenth Street Baptist Church during the twenty-fourth nightly rally "of the

Birmingham citizens working and marching against segregation." King, Abernathy and Shuttlesworth were on the platform. Wilkins "hailed the work of Birmingham citizens who defied police dogs and other intimidation to protest segregation."[106]

With King in Birmingham, the world was watching. The motel became a revolving door for celebrities, politicians and movement supporters. "It was fantastic," Ernest said. "They were all coming in to help the movement: Joan Baez, Bobby Kennedy. We had people from the Office of Civil Rights, the FBI there at all times."

Even Young had to admit that "it would have been much harder to run a movement in Birmingham without Gaston's motel and his restaurant."[107]

"I walked out every day, and there in the courtyard were people who would be internationally famous," Stephanie remembered. "Dr. King would tap me on the head and say, 'How are you doing?' I saw all these people daily—Andrew Young, Wyatt Tee Walker."

"They had these huge concerts to fundraise for the movement, and they all stayed at the Gaston Motel," Stephanie said. "Me, being the hostess and switchboard operator, I would see them all: Ike and Tina Turner, Johnny Mathis. All those people were just all around. It was a very interesting time."

The Gibsons remembered once when Stephanie served singer Johnny Mathis's dinner. She gave him his plate but forgot an essential tool. "My parents tell the story that he said, 'Darling, I can certainly eat this barbecue with my fingers, but I don't know about this coleslaw. Can you get me a fork?'"

The motel's courtyard was where King would hold his daily press conferences. The area would be filled with reporters from around the world, supporters and locals. They all hung on the words of King, Shuttlesworth and others.

"We had to provide phones and that nature so they could scramble to get the news back to their agencies so that people could report their stories," Ernest said.

There were any number of people from outside the United States, he said, people from Canada, England, any number of foreign countries. "It was good for the movement and basically a strategy of Dr. King for exposure, to create awareness of what was happening in Birmingham to let everyone know about the movement."

At one time, they had one hundred rabbis come down and donate money for the cause, he said.

The visitors included performers, politicians and celebrities of all kinds: Nina Simone, Joe Lewis, Jackie Robinson, Ray Charles and his whole band.

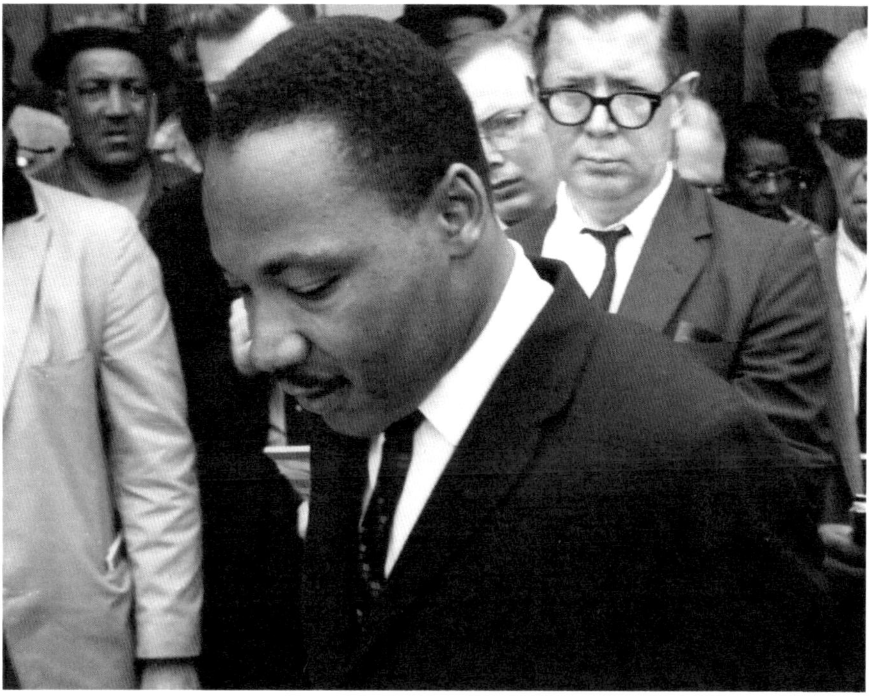

Martin Luther King Jr. speaks at a press conference at the Gaston Motel. *Courtesy of Birmingham Civil Rights Institute.*

Roy Wilkins was in and out of the motel. Constance Baker Motley was always there. Wiley Branton Sr., the attorney for the Little Rock Nine, was there, too. Stephanie later married his son, Wiley Branton Jr.

"Gaston was beginning to resemble Grand Central Station at rush hour," Andrew Young wrote. "The motel bubbled with activity and discussions on a twenty-four hour basis. It had become the site of a national meeting and greeting convention, an ongoing debating society on the pertinent questions of the movement, a place where supporters might meet or see or talk with Martin if he was available, a continuing education seminar on the movement conducted by Wyatt for visiting reporters and supporters, and a magnet for the curious celebrity hounds."[108]

"After the mass meetings, our staff would return to Martin's room at Gaston's for a time of fellowship," Young wrote. "It was in these late night meetings that the real decisions and directions of the campaign were determined."[109]

"And, of course, there was food—Martin loved to eat—fried chicken or barbecued ribs, or both," Young said. "I learned to love the ribs: there was something about the elemental act of chewing on bones that brought one back to basics and seemed to encourage honest searching among staff, discouraging the usual ego battles or jockeying for favor with Martin. It's hard to put on airs when you in the middle of eating messy ribs."[110]

During the day, King was often quiet and reflective, Young wrote, "but at night he came alive and dominated the gatherings with a mixture of playful preaching and joke telling, a side of his personality he rarely displayed in public...His manner set the tone for a relaxed analysis of the day's activities and a leisurely charting of strategy for the next few days. Often it was 2:00 a.m. or later before we began to drift off to bed, leaving Martin, Ralph, and A.D. the last ones to turn in. It was these fellowships I remember most about that time. They were sheer joy, and Martin's energy and charisma were as dominant in this kind of small gathering as on any major speaking platform."[111]

YOU NEVER KNEW WHO YOU WOULD SEE AT THE GASTON

"Everybody who was anybody was there," said Dale Long. "Even the Anglo reporters and photographers couldn't stay at the Tutwiler and such if they didn't want their equipment torn up."

Long also said he had fond memories of comedian Dick Gregory being at the motel and recalls his dad bringing Gregory home. "I remember listening to the stories. It made such an impression."

Long also recalls one day seeing a nice car drive up to the motel. "It was Sam Cooke," he said."He was sitting there like he was all that and then some."

Photographer Robert Adelman came to the motel because he was covering the Student Nonviolent Coordinating Committee and the Congress of Racial Equality (SNCC). "We heard there were big doings in Birmingham," he said. He hitched a ride down there and stayed at the motel because he refused to patronize the Tutwiler Hotel or other white hotel that would not allow blacks."I was trying to fight segregation, not support it," he said.

He was traveling with fellow photographer Bruce Davidson. The next morning, he went onto the restaurant patio and had a breakfast of eggs and grits in the outdoor courtyard. "Sitting at one of the tables was Dr. King," he remembered. He joined him, and so did twenty-three-year-old folk singer Joan Baez, as well as some reporter from *Time* magazine.

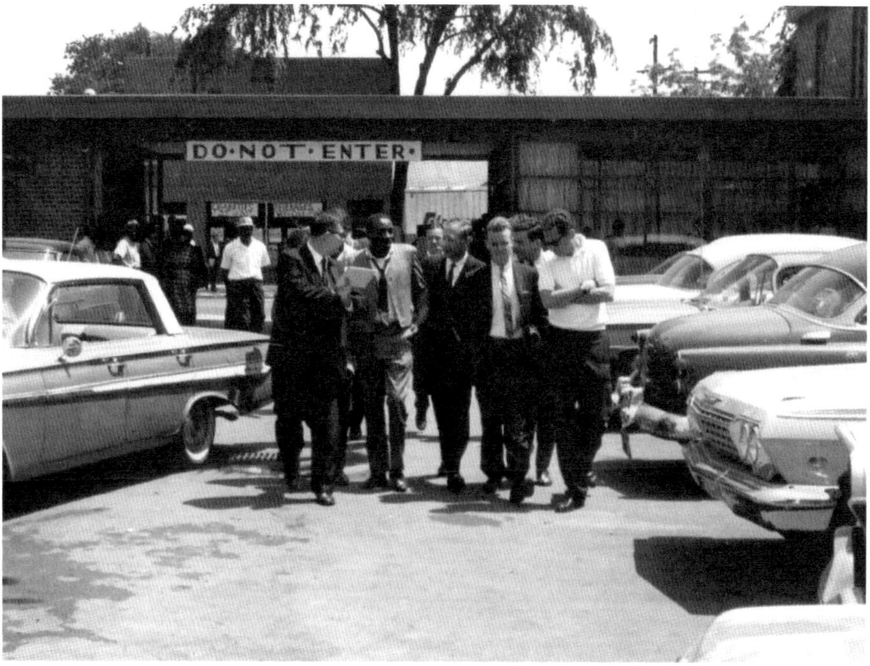

Comedian Dick Gregory walking with a group. *Courtesy of Birmingham Civil Rights Institute.*

Baez was mercilessly needling the reporter, Adelman remembered. She told him that reporters thought they knew everything. "She was very young and had a lot of attitude about the press," he said. "She gave the reporter a hard time."

Dr. King laughed and laughed, Adelman remembered. "He was soft-spoken. He looked you right in the eye and gave you his full attention."

Baez was in town to perform at Miles College for a Sunday, May 5 concert. During the event, she spotted a woman with a bandage and stopped to acknowledge her: "I hope that doesn't hurt too bad."

Among her playlist, she sang "We Shall Overcome."[112]

Adelman heard Dr. King speak at Sixteenth Street Church. He was also there when some of the protesting took place. "The demonstrations were hair-raising, very frightening," he said and added that he ended up staying only a few days. "I wasn't hanging around."

The Gibsons could understand why. "As I look back now, it was very exciting," Ernest said. "At the same time, it was really tough."

Especially when guests did not pay their bills, he said. "I never had any problems with the movement paying," he said. "The problem I had with

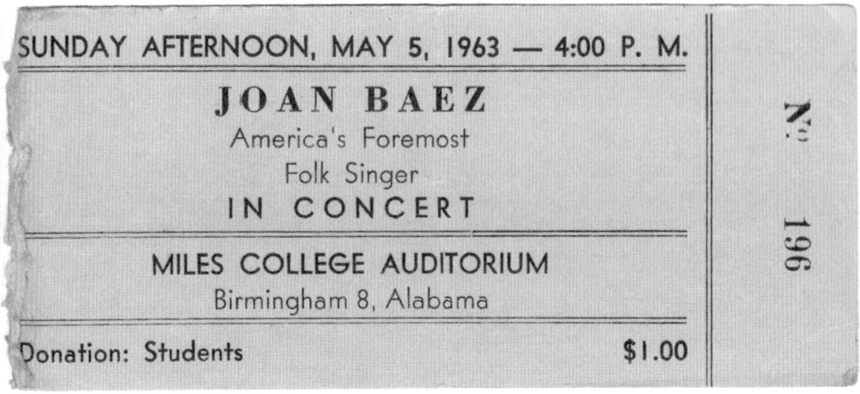

A ticket to a Joan Baez concert at Miles College. *Courtesy of Birmingham Civil Rights Institute.*

people paying were people coming out of New York and entertainers. They would come in to perform at rallies, stay in the motel and do their performances for Martin and the group."

He said that the Godfather of Soul, James Brown, and several others checked in and left without taking care of the bill, owing Gibson up in the thousands.

Washington remembers spotting a young Jesse Jackson outside the motel. Washington was teaching at Booker T. Washington Business College across the street. His students also saw Jackson and wanted a chance to go over and meet him.

"I introduced myself," Washington said. He told the activist about his students wanting to meet him, but Jackson sent him back with his tail tucked beneath him. "He said, 'I don't have time for that,'" Washington remembered. "[Jackson] was standing on the side wanting to be seen."

TENDING TO THE MOVEMENT

The Gibsons' lives became enmeshed with those of the movement leaders, they said. Even little things became a concern for them, like the time King came out of jail and was looking very unkempt.

Gibson told the preacher, "You need to wash up. You still need a haircut."

"Where can I get a haircut?" King asked. Gibson took him to a local barber. The customers were so excited, Gibson remembered.

"He talked to everybody and then said, 'We are going to go.' I said, 'Wait a minute. Let me pay the person,' because Martin never had any money and never [had to] pay for anything. He just go get what he want and walk out."

King said, "You've got to pay for that?"

The barber said, "No."

King said, "I told you you ain't got to pay. It's just a haircut."

Then, King went around and spoke to everyone and hugged everybody, Gibson remembered.

Gibson also recalled a time when he tried to help King get more comfortable for his protest work. "Martin would always dress nice—nice suits and ties and shirts," Gibson said. "But when he returned from marching, he'd look like he had been sleeping on the railroad tracks. They beat him. He was bloody, dirty, needed a shave and all that. I always liked to wear, when I was working the yard in Arkansas, coveralls. I said to Martin, 'I am getting tired of you and these suits you are wearing. We gonna take these shirts off and suits off. I got him some overalls.'"

"Abernathy got mad, said, 'Where is mine?' I said, 'Hell, you are too fat. I don't have anything big enough to fit you,'" Gibson said. "You would see [King] in jail with those jumpsuits. Those were mine."

Time for a New Direction

After spending days and weeks covering the happenings of the movement, the local and national media began to lose interest. King and his group felt that something extraordinary needed to take place to continue the momentum of national interest. Jim Bevel, director of direct action and nonviolent education for the SCLC, had the solution.

He would recruit children to march for freedom and fill up the jails. The youngsters were not at risk of losing jobs for participating in the movement. They had the energy and were ready to go. Though apprehensive, King greenlighted the recruitment of youngsters for what would be called D-Day. The plan would be to get the children to fill the jails.

"The children's crusade was a big thing," Stephanie said. "Any parent would want to shelter their kids, but the crusade was a game changer."

Stephanie was anxious about it and wanted to participate.

"Dad, I am going to march," Gibson remembered her saying.

"OK, but I am going to march beside you with my gun," he told her.

"Daddy, you cannot do that," she told him.

On Thursday, May 2, the children's marches began. Excited youngsters gladly stood in line to march for freedom, and Shelley Stewart, who had learned from King how to rouse a crowd toward action, was on the radio giving code language to eager listeners.

"Bring your toothbrush," he would tell them. "You ought to brush your teeth."

That was code that they should expect to spend the night in jail.

Thousands of excited youngsters packed the streets and readied themselves for a nonviolent fight for freedom. Connor used dogs and water hoses to try to deter them, and images of this reached around the world. Viewers were horrified to see how people in Birmingham attacked and arrested children who simply wanted freedom.

The jails began to fill, and still more and more children came out each day. On Monday, May 6, comedian and activist Dick Gregory led about eight hundred marchers who had to be bused to the Alabama State Fairgrounds because there was no availability in the jam-packed jails.

The next day, Clarence B. Hanson Jr., publisher of the *Birmingham News*, sent a telegram to President John F. Kennedy. It was published on the front page of the newspaper. The headline spliced across the top was "A Telegram to the President":

> *Dear Mr. President,*
>
> *...Demonstrations have been unleashed in Birmingham by an organization which seems deliberately intent, having created open turmoil, on continuing it indefinitely.*
>
> *Mr. President, if these were white marches, demonstrations, open defiances of uniformed law officers, we believe your Administration would have taken vigorous action to discourage them.*
>
> *...The way to eliminate such threat of violence is to prevent large crowds gathering.*
>
> *...It would grieve you deeply if injury or death should result—particularly to Negro school children who are being cynically used in this needless day-after-day provocation.*
>
> *But, Mr. President, Negroes are gathered, are excited by speeches, and then are sent boldly into the streets where they openly taunt police and provoke not only the white community but the very law itself.*
>
> *...We ask you, Sir, to use the influence of your office to end this open law violation and provocation.*

> *...White respect for law, however, is assuredly damaged when Negroes seem with relative impunity to be able to foster open law defiance.*
>
> *...I now call on Dr.* [Martin Luther] *King again, in the name of properly, peacefully achieved civil rights for all citizens, Negro and white, to do his part to bring about an end to disorder in the streets and give Birmingham citizens, Negro and white, their opportunity to achieve the ends that Mr. Kennedy has set forth.*
>
> *That is the "picture" today, Mr. President. But apparently if there is to be order, and respect for the law, and proper procedure through the courts as well as sincere white effort to meet this problem cooperatively, you, Sir, must be the one to bring it.*

Later, Kennedy's associate press secretary, Andrew Hatcher, said there would be no comment to the telegram: "It has become part of our study of this thing. We are not sitting idly by. We just can't say anything."

That same day, Shuttlesworth was injured during a protest. He was knocked to the ground and had to be hospitalized. King wrote that Connor

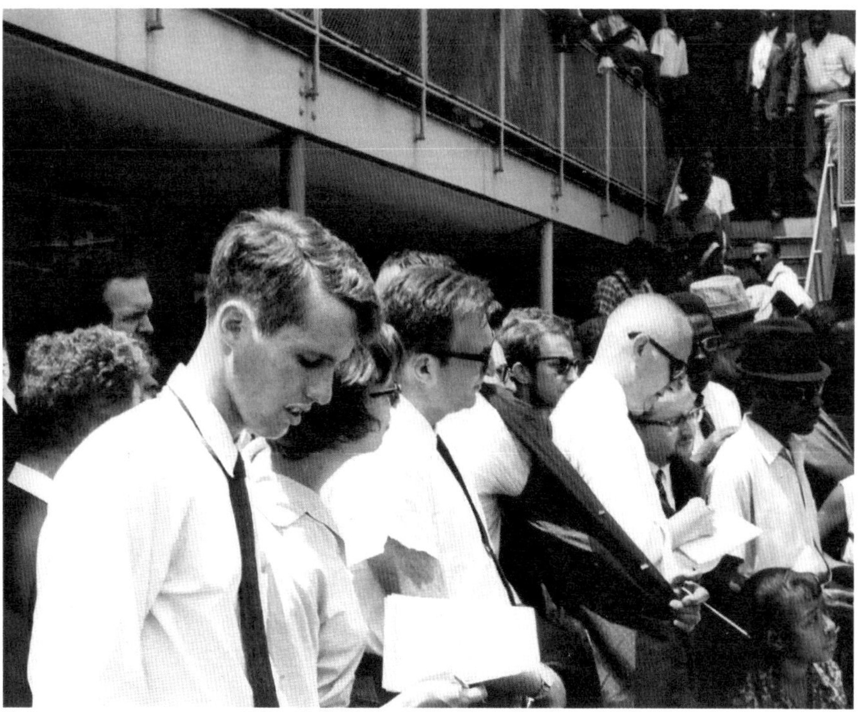

A press conference held at the Gaston Motel. *Courtesy of Birmingham Civil Rights Institute.*

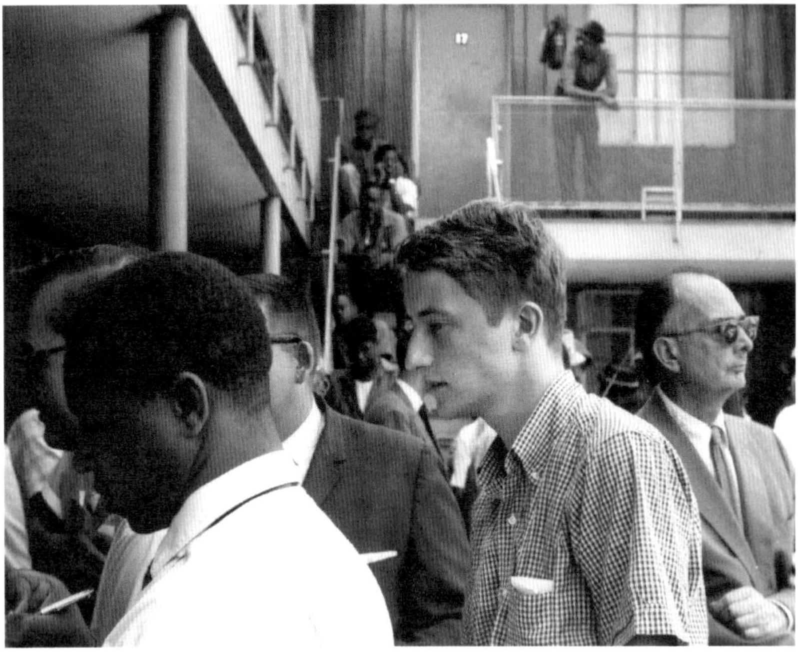

Press conference. *Courtesy of Birmingham Civil Rights Institute.*

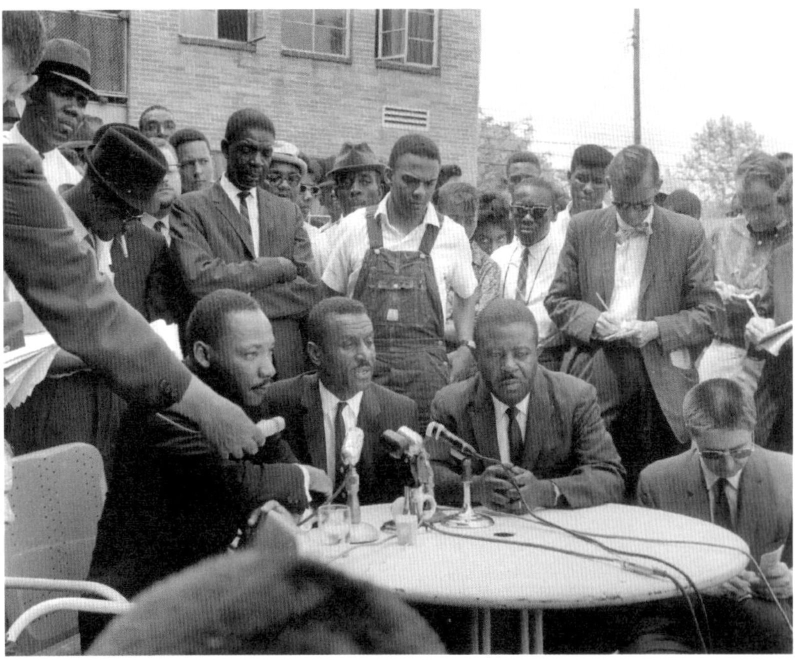

Seated, left to right: Martin Luther King Jr., Ralph Abernathy and Andrew Young. *Photo by Chris McNair of Chris McNair Studios.*

was heard saying that he wished Shuttlesworth had been carried away in a hearse. On that Wednesday, May 8, the black leaders negotiated a truce to end the demonstrations. Shuttlesworth was not involved in that discussion, so he checked himself out of the hospital to demand more than what was agreed upon.

With Shuttlesworth's input, a new agreement was made, and he announced it from the Gaston courtyard. A pact of peace had been reached, and the business community agreed to desegregate its lunch counters, restrooms, etc.; to hire Negroes as clerks and salespeople within sixty days; to work on the release of jailed protestors; and to establish communications between whites and Negroes. After making his speech, Shuttlesworth, still weary from his injuries, got up to leave and fainted.

Chapter 8

THE LAST STRAW

Dr. King was on a plane headed to Birmingham and didn't have a ride from the airport. Wyatt Tee Walker, who was out of town, called the Gibsons for help, and Carolyn was dispatched to pick him up. She had a petite 1963 white Thunderbird sports car at the time. King was amused by the ride, Carolyn remembered, and said that every time he was at the airport he would like Mrs. Gibson to pick him up.

And she did.

"That ended up not being a good thing for me," she said. "It became a marked car."

During that time, the Gibsons lived on Dynamite Hill near Arthur Shores and his family. One particular night, Carolyn headed home to relieve her babysitter, a high school student who lived nearby. She went home, picked up the girl and drove her four blocks down the hill. While driving back home, Carolyn noticed that a police vehicle was following and tailed her right into the driveway.

When Carolyn parked, Stephanie watched out the window as the officers took her mother from her car and put her in a paddy wagon. Carolyn yelled to Stephanie to call her dad and tell him what was happening.

"We got the bitch, King's wife," she heard an officer say into the radio. Carolyn said they must have assumed she was Coretta Scott King because she and the woman looked similar and also because she was often riding in the car with King, as she was his designated driver from the airport.

For the next three or four hours, Carolyn was transferred from one paddy wagon to the next as they picked up drunkards, pickpockets, you name it.

By the time she got to the jail, her husband and his attorney were there. The supposed charge was speeding, she said, and the policemen fingerprinted her and prepared her to be put in a cell.

She did not go to jail that night but did have to appear in court. Since there was no foundation to the charge, she said, the judge dismissed the case.

That was not the end of the terror, according to Carolyn.

"We got threats at our home," Ernest remembered. "We received threats every single day at the motel and where we lived. We received so many that we sold our home and converted two of the motel suites into a home. If we are going to die, we are going to all die together."

For Stephanie, living in the motel put them at the center of all the action. "All I had to do was stand on the corner and watch," she recalled. The images of children being sprayed in Kelly Ingram Park and police clubbing protestors with Billy clubs being shown on the nightly news were nothing new to her; she was an eyewitness to it all.

"Things were going so fast and so furious; things were happening every day," Carolyn said. The motel adjusted its hours to accommodate the movement in many ways, she said. "We were open late at night. One of our main purposes after a while of being open late was to accept all the leaders and movement people who had been jailed."

Normally, the Birmingham police would release jailed protesters in the early hours of morning or late at night, she said. Once released, the folks would usually gravitate to the motel and be hungry. "We would feed the whole group," Carolyn said. "Martin would meet with them and conduct kind of a session to figure out what they were going to do next."

Late night meetings were commonplace for King and his group, Ernest said, and as the motel manager, on many occasions, he had a front-row seat. "I was the only one allowed in to serve them," he said of the men's evening work sessions. "I did not allow anyone because we didn't want information to get out, but it was getting out; not from my people. It was getting out from some of the people in the movement."

The custom was that they would come into the restaurant from a mass meeting at one of the churches in the city or the suburbs and Gibson would serve them food. In case they needed anything, Gibson would stay, sit off to the side doing bookkeeping. He overheard a lot, he said. "All of the movement and all of the schedules and everything."

"The meetings were very tense, argumentative," he said. "They had different points of view. When it all was said and done, when they all came out, they would have a unified front. Martin wanted certain things.

Shuttlesworth wanted certain things. There were always good discussions; some were arguments.

Typically, the meetings would end with the group linking arms and singing "We Shall Overcome." In between verses of the chorus, someone in the circle would chime in a prayer request or make a statement.

"Martin, one night, called me," Gibson said. "The meeting was over. He said, 'Gip, get on down here and get in this circle.' He said, 'Get next to me. You are in this movement.'"

The group began to sing, and one by one, members took turns saying something in between the chorus.

Gibson was standing beside King when he began to speak. "There is a Judas among us," King said, "and I want that person to get out of the movement." Gibson was stunned by the words coming out of King's mouth. "I want all of you to know that things are not going so well. And if you are not ready to die for this movement, I want you to get out of this circle. Get out and don't come back."

"If I had hair on my body, it would be standing up," Gibson said. "I was actually shaking. I realized the man, the dynamics of this man called Martin. Although I had worked at Tuskegee and helped with marches, etc., I joined the movement that night."

"I think I got religion," Gibson continued. "I cannot even explain it today. I got to the point, I am ready to die and I believed in him so much."

As the days went on, it seemed Gibson would be faced with that possibility. With so much going on, Ernest decided to send his family on a trip to visit relatives in Little Rock while he stayed behind. Mother's Day weekend was coming up, and Carolyn wanted to see her mom.

The Saturday night before Mother's Day, Gibson was swamped. "I was operating the telephones that night; we were short on everybody," he said.

He got a bomb threat that evening, which wasn't unusual, he said. "We had a standard procedure for when we got a call. We were supposed to call the county, the state troopers, the FBI. We did this all day."

Usually the perpetrator would call and say, "We are going to bomb you and shoot the place up," Gibson remembered, but it was always just a threat.

Just before midnight on May 11, though, across town someone threw a bomb at the home of King's brother, the Reverend A.D. King. It blew off part of the house. A.D.'s wife was sitting in the living room when she heard a car speeding by. The younger King, who was pastor of First Baptist Church of Ensley, and their five children were in the back of the house in bed. The front walls of the home were blown down and the interior walls

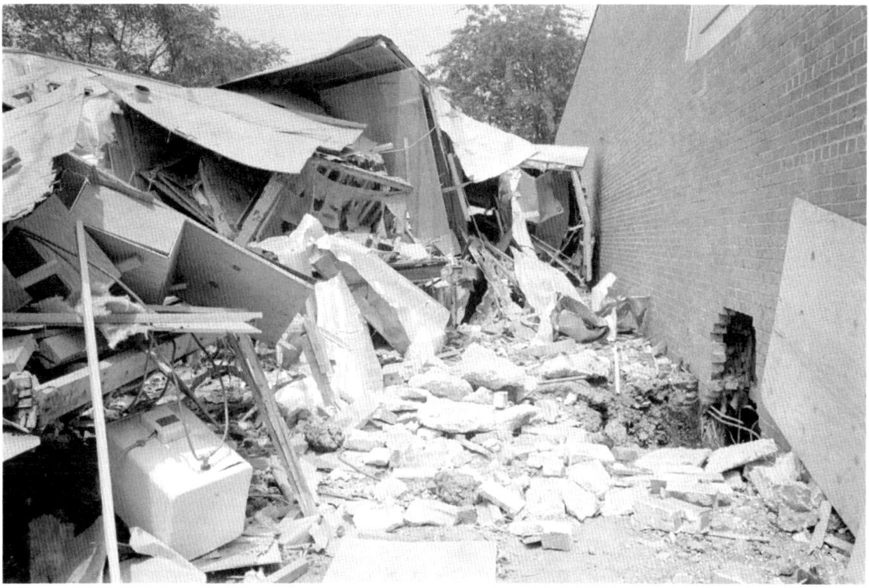

The aftermath of the Gaston Motel Bombing. *Courtesy of Birmingham Civil Rights Institute.*

badly damaged. The bomb also left a four- by five-foot-wide hole in the Kings' yard.

No one was hurt because of the house's structure, King later told the *New York Times*: "It's brick," he said of his home at 721 Twelfth Avenue. "That's the only thing that saved us."

Minutes after the bomb at King's home, around 11:58 p.m., sticks of dynamite were thrown at the Gaston Motel. Folks in the restaurant began to scream, Gibson remembered. "Some started to run into the street," he told the *Times*. "Before the dust from the explosion had settled, Negroes began streaming into the street from taverns, night spots and small groceries."

Witnesses said the perpetrators were four men and were believed to be in a 1962 automobile. Three women were injured: Lola May Harris, Ruth Sawyer and Annie Maxton.

The bomb was "placed as to kill or seriously wound anyone who might have been in Room 30—my room," Dr. Martin Luther King Jr. wrote.[113] "Evidently the would-be assassins did not know I was in Atlanta that night."

Not only was Gibson glad that King was out of town, but he was relieved his wife was, too. "I would have lost my wife had she been there," Gibson said. "At that time of day she normally did the bookkeeping and payroll." She would have been sitting in the office just beneath Room 30, right where the bomb was thrown.

George Washington remembers that night. He was in Liberty Supermarket with his best friend, Leon Brown. While stocking their grocery cart with various fruit juices for alcoholic drinks, Brown told Washington he was getting married. "I told him he had to be crazy," Washington said. "We were eighteen, nineteen years old."

Liberty was the grocery store where "Lay" worked; he was a security guard who had tried for years to get on the police force. "They never would let him on," Washington said. Blacks were given every excuse in the book why they weren't allowed, Washington said, and joked that if you were black, "you had to be a Harvard graduate to be a police officer."

But that night's bombing was no joke.

"We all felt the bomb go off," Washington said. "That was Fifth Avenue and Thirteenth Street, two blocks away."

Rand Jimerson, who was a white boy living in Homewood just outside Birmingham at the time, remembered that when he heard the news, he thought about how he and his dad had just visited the motel two days before. His preacher/activist dad, Norman C. Jimerson, had driven him to the motel the Friday before Mother's Day to drop off a package. His father was the director of the Alabama Council on Human Relations. His role was to provide education about race relations.

"He talked about the motel as the gathering place," Jimerson remembered of his father's talks.

His dad stopped at the Gaston, and young Jimerson stayed in the car but remembered seeing people dressed in "African-type clothing—long white robes and colorful dashikis. It seemed to be exotic," he remembered. "Then, two days later, it was bombed. I had just been there."

"The bombing had been well timed," King wrote.[114] "The bars in the Negro district close at midnight, and the bombs exploded just as some of Birmingham's Saturday night drinkers came out of the bars. Thousands of Negroes poured into the streets."[115]

This time, though, they weren't as long-suffering as they had been in the past. They were mad. Local musician John Springer noticed that a crowd started to gather. "I saw what I never thought I'd see in my life," he said. "A man took his hand, pulled a brick out the wall and threw it into the window of a white business."

The bombings were the last straw, he said. "It's like this: if you are already mad at your husband and he comes up to you and slaps you, you are ready to do him in. We were already mad."

About 1,500 people gathered on this Mother's Day early morning. Some began taking knives to the tires of the police vehicles. Sticks were thrown. Cars were overturned. King wrote that he believed the bombers wanted the people to riot.[116]

The crowd began to shout, "Kill 'em! Kill 'em!" according to Claude Sitton, a reporter for the *New York Times*.

Alabama state troopers, who had been in town earlier for the children's march, were called back to the city after news of the bombing.

The crowd began to swell to 2,500. Law enforcement fought back, including hurting innocent Negroes. Their acts included "the clubbing of the diminutive Anne Walker, Wyatt's wife, as she was about to enter her husband's quarters at the partially bombed out Gaston Motel."[117]

Wyatt took his wife to the hospital, and when he returned, he tried to encourage peace. He wrapped a white handkerchief around his wrist and waved it to the crowd. He pleaded with them to stop the violence but was hit by a brick.

"They started it," the crowd was reported as yelling.

King's brother A.D. arrived and tried to help calm the crowd. "We're not mad anymore," he told them. "We're saying, 'Father, forgive them for they know not what they do.'"

Twenty-eight blocks were sealed off, and no one was allowed in or out. When all was said and done, about fifty people were injured, including a taxi driver and policeman who were stabbed, according to Sitton's report.

Birmingham commissioner Art Hanes was venomous: "The nigger King ought to be investigated by the Attorney General and the White House," he said but offered no faith in Attorney General Robert Kennedy. "I hope every drop of blood that's spilled he tastes in his throat, and I hope he chokes on it."

Sitton also reported that someone came out of the entranceway of the motel and shouted across the street to the law enforcement, "We don't have guns. Why do you have guns?"

To no avail, shortly thereafter, state troopers charged the motel. "Negroes fled in terror as they were clubbed with gun butts and nightsticks," Sitton wrote. "The 'thonk' of clubs striking heads could be heard across the street."

When the sun finally rose, a young Dale Long had no idea what had happened overnight. All he knew was that it was Sunday morning, which meant he and his brother would usually awaken to the smell of coffee and pancakes. On this day, however, people were in the house—white people, he said.

When he opened his eyes, a white man with a plaid shirt and jeans and a pistol on his hip was in his room. His brother jumped into the bed with him. "We knew something was wrong," he said. "The gun set things off for us. We were afraid to get out of bed."

Then, his mother walked in. She told them that the men in the house were with the FBI and reporters were there as well. She told them that the motel had been bombed.

"We broke away," he said. Long and his brother wanted to make sure their father, who had worked at the motel the night before, was OK.

The boys' mother also told them that Reverend A.D. King's home had been bombed. The King boys were Dale and his brother's friends. He was relieved to know that they weren't hurt.

Dr. King's brother A.D. called Martin to tell him about the devastation.

"Then, in the background as he talked, I heard a swelling burst of beautiful song," Dr. King wrote.[118] People began to sing "We Shall Overcome." "I marveled that in a moment of such tragedy the Negro could still express himself with hope and with faith." [119]

Dr. King said that people showed the support of the movement by sending letters, donations, piggy banks and checks to the motel.[120] The bombing just inconvenienced the Gaston for a little bit but did not stop it, the Gibsons said.

With all that was going on, there was an issue about whether the motel bomb threat had been received by the FBI. "I personally called the FBI, everybody, but the FBI from Washington said I never called," Gibson said. "I think that was in the *New York Times* that I refuted the fact that they said that I did not call."

That made Carolyn nervous. "So you can see my tension," she said. "I felt, 'Now you have refuted the FBI, we need to get out of here.'"

Even after the bombing, though, many staff and locals weren't afraid to continue patronizing the motel. So much security was added after that, Springer said, both A.G. Gaston's security people plus a lot of plainclothes men.

But there were other things to fear.

On May 15, 2,500 members of the Ku Klux Klan burned two twenty-foot crosses minutes outside Birmingham in Bessemer to denounce integration. The area blacks felt more was brewing. That same day, Dick Gregory claimed to have been beaten in a Birmingham jail.

Days later, on May 18, it was reported that ex–heavyweight boxing champion Floyd Patterson and baseball great Jackie Robinson flew into town to meet with King and Abernathy to urge Negroes to avoid violence.

But while they were preaching nonviolence, violent acts continued to plague the nonviolent.

While living in Birmingham, Stephanie had made lots of friends, including Denise McNair, daughter of Chris and Maxine McNair. Their parents were dear friends, too, the Gibsons said. Chris McNair was a young entrepreneur and took a lot of pictures of the movement.

On Sunday morning, September 15, Stephanie asked if she could go to Sixteenth Street Baptist Church. It was Children's Day, and she wanted to see her friend Denise participate in the program. Ernest and Carolyn agreed. As Stephanie was preparing to get dressed, however, a bomb at the church exploded.

"Everyone heard it," Stephanie said, "and it was sadly familiar, because you knew probably what had happened."

"It was terrifying," Long said. "You quickly had to learn how to conduct yourselves in Birmingham. Your parents couldn't do it for you."

He and his brother Ken were in the church during the explosion. His dad was at work at the motel when it happened. The elder Long ran toward the church praying that his sons were okay. "I had never seen my dad run before," Long said. "I found Ken, and we were standing there holding on to each other."

By the time his dad made it to the corner, police had roped off the area, Long remembered. "Dad said, 'Those are my boys, you gotta move.'"

His father took them to the office in the Gaston Motel. He looked them over to make sure they were all right. Then, he tried to call his wife to let her know that Long and his brother were OK. They couldn't make the call because there was pandemonium, Long said. There were two to three pay phones in the lobby, and the many journalists were trying to call in to report the bombing. A fight broke out over the phones. Black and white reporters were coming to blows.

"The phone kept ringing," Long remembered. "I didn't know anyone had been killed. Bombings were a way of life."

Then, the news came. The victims were Cynthia Wesley, Carole Robertson and Addie Mae Collins, all fourteen, and little Denise McNair, who was just eleven.

"We knew everyone in the church," Long said. "Carole's funeral was at St. John's on Tuesday. The others were Wednesday."

Long remembered the funeral for the three girls. "For a moment, I am watching three bodies," he said. Then, he spotted King. "I [had seen] him on TV, never ten feet away. He was looking at me."

Carolyn and Ernest were devastated for their friends the McNairs. At the time, the McNairs had only one child. "They did not plan to have more children," Carolyn said, "but when Denise died, they quickly decided to try again," Carolyn said.

The day Denise was killed, Carolyn was one day out of the hospital after having had a miscarriage. She had a lot of maternity clothes leftover. "Later on, when I found out Mrs. McNair was pregnant, I sent her the maternity clothes," she said. "That made me feel very good that I was able to share with her."

With everything that was going on, Gaston was not happy with all the movement people coming in and out of the motel, Gibson said. "Gaston came to me and said, 'Ernie, too many of these white folks are hanging around this motel and coming in from Washington, D.C. I just don't like this, and I don't like that King,'" Gibson remembered. "'You have to get them out of here.'"

"I said, 'Whether you like it or not, there is nothing you can do about it. Two things: We have an agreement and this is my motel, and I am running it as a first-class business. Secondly, this is Alabama. I can't tell white people they can't come in here and eat at my motel. Now they can tell me not to eat downtown. Yeah, there are white folks living here. Whether you know it or not, Bobby Kennedy spent two nights here.'

"Gaston said, 'Well, this is still my property.' He was very arrogant, and I was on his list then," Gibson said. "We then began to prepare to try to get out of this business," he said. "It was more difficult to get out than get in."

"Gaston was happy for me to get out," Gibson said, but "he gave me a hard time. When you are in business like that, you just don't walk away."

The tables had turned for Gibson, who had been one of Gaston's friends. "A lot of those boys in his organization didn't like it because I was favored," he said. "I went up in the penthouse, got massages and steam baths. I was 'the best thing since sliced bread,'" Gibson remembered. Because of that, he met resistance with several members of Gaston's leadership. "They were fighting me. They were poisoning Dr. Gaston against me. They were saying that I was with Dr. King, and I would say, 'Yes, I am with him 150 percent.'"

Ernest and his family ended their tenure at the Gaston Motel and moved out. While they worked out severing ties with Gaston, they moved into the old home of a friend who had just built a new house. Ernest began working as the assistant to the president of Miles College, as well as at a country club over the mountain.

In May 1964, Stephanie's parents sent her and her sister to New Jersey to stay with family. "It was during that time that my parents said we were moving," she said. "I don't have a clear memory of returning to Birmingham, but I know that when I did, it was to pack and leave. There was no grand celebration. I was gone."

With the help of a local attorney, the Gibsons were emancipated and left Birmingham by the summer of 1964.

"It was almost two years of not a good situation," Carolyn said. "It was a relief to walk away. A relief from all the stress."

"In spite of all the things that happened, the one thing we learned from the experience, it made us stronger people," Carolyn said. "We did not leave with a chip on our shoulder. We weren't bitter."

They moved to Illinois.

Chapter 9

MUSIC IN THE AIR

It was the place to do. It was like Cheers, *where everybody knows your name.*
—George A. Washington

With the Gibsons in Illinois and the legal matters regarding their departure resolved, the restaurant and motel saw several changes in management. Among those who, at one time, took the helm as the manager of the restaurant and lounge was T.A. Peevy Jr., a dapper army veteran with good business acumen. Peevy had worked as a debit-building agent with Booker T. Washington Insurance Company. After only nine weeks in that position, he was transferred to the Internal Auditing Department. Next, he was given the task to run the Gaston.

"I find it very interesting and challenging," Peevy said of his new role.[121]

The Birmingham native received his BS degree in business management from Miles College. He was a member of Omega Psi Phi Fraternity, Inc. and had also done graduate work at the University of Maryland.

Gaston also rehired Arzell "Skippie" Skipwith to serve as the official hostess of the restaurant and lounge. She had worked as a greeter for the Bob Savoy Café for twenty years and as a cashier for the Gaston Motel Restaurant from 1956 to 1962. The "reclamation of Miss Skipwith brings to the restaurant and general public an extensive background of training and experience," Gaston told *Birmingham World*.

"Miss Skipwith has garnered a vast number of friends and satisfied patrons, resulting from her pleasing personality and immeasurable service." A bartender nicknamed "Sister" was part of the team, too.

T. A. Peevy Jr. Named Manager Of Gaston Motel, Restaurant

"I find it very interesting and challenging," is the way T. A. Peevy, Jr., sums up his new position as manager of the A. G. Gaston Motel and Restaurant.

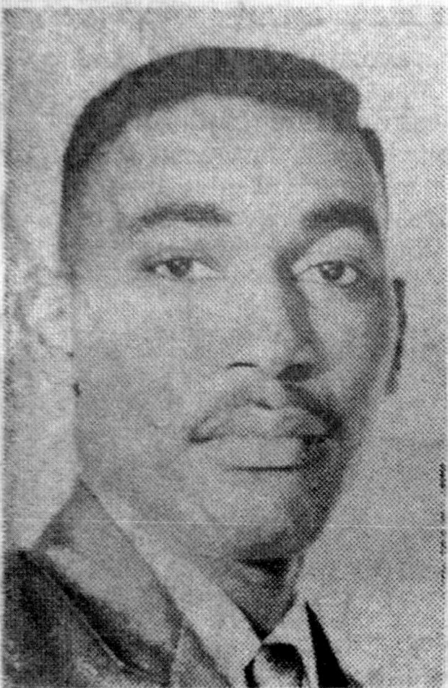

A. A. PEEVY

The announcement said: "For the past month Mr. Peevy has demonstrated that he has what it takes to serve in this dual capacity."

Mr. Peevy began his employment with the Smith and Gaston Interest as a debit-building agent for the Booker T. Washington Insurance Company. After nine weeks, he was transferred to the Internal Auditing Department.

Mr. Peevy is a native of Birmingham, Ala. He attended the Birmingham Public Schools and earned his B. S. Degree from Miles College in Business Administration. He did graduate work at the University of Maryland, while serving his country in the United States Army. He taught in the Birmingham Public School Sstem prior to his employment with Smith and Gaston Interest.

He is a member of Our Lady of Fatima Catholic Church of which the Rev. Paul Downey is the pastor. Mr. Peevy is a member of Alpha Kappa Mu National Honor Society. He holds membership in the Omega Psi Phi Fraternity, Inc. and the 18th Street Branch YMCA.

Additionally, he makes his home with his parents, Mr. and Mrs. T. A. Peevy, Sr., of 1012 No. Sixth St.

Birmingham World news article. *Courtesy of Birmingham Civil Rights Institute.*

With his new team in place, Gaston began an advertising campaign in *Birmingham World*, touting his chicken dinners and such. Gaston also became more strategic with marketing language, branding the place as an "after the theater retreat" "where fine food is served with distinction."

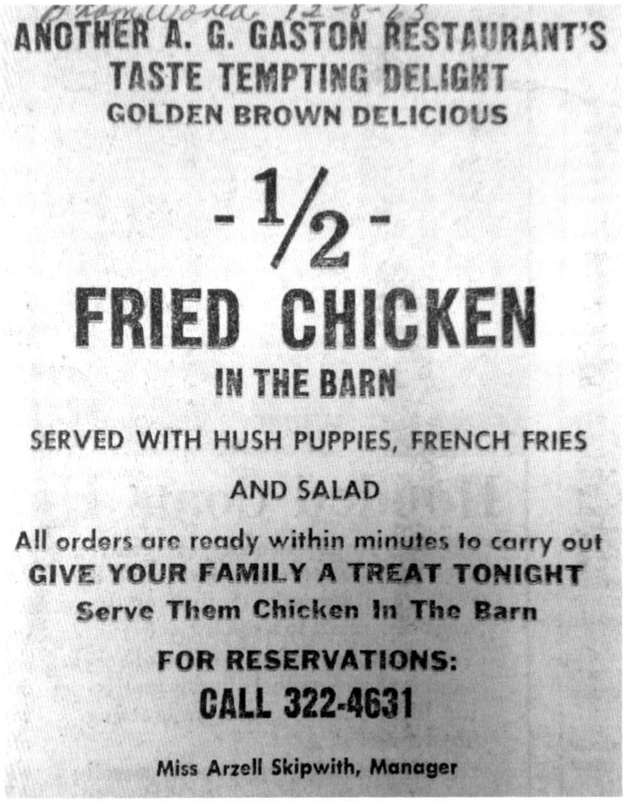

Left: *Birmingham World* advertisement. *Courtesy of Birmingham Civil Rights Institute.*

Below, left: *Birmingham World* advertisement. *Courtesy of Birmingham Civil Rights Institute.*

Below, right: *Birmingham World* advertisement. *Courtesy of Birmingham Civil Rights Institute.*

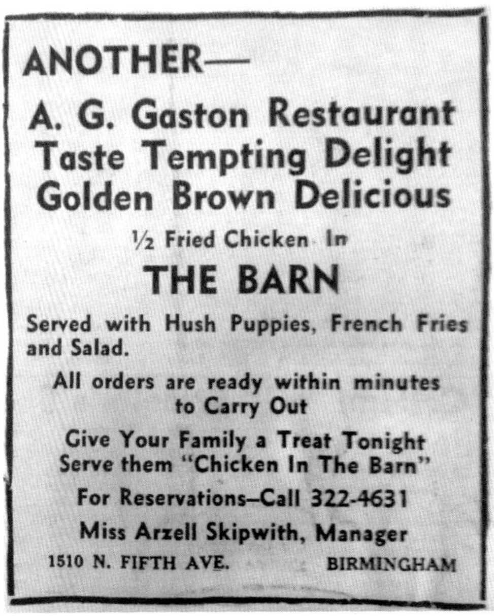

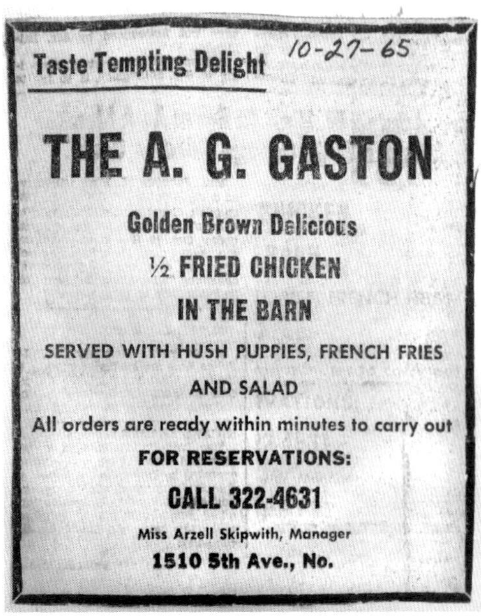

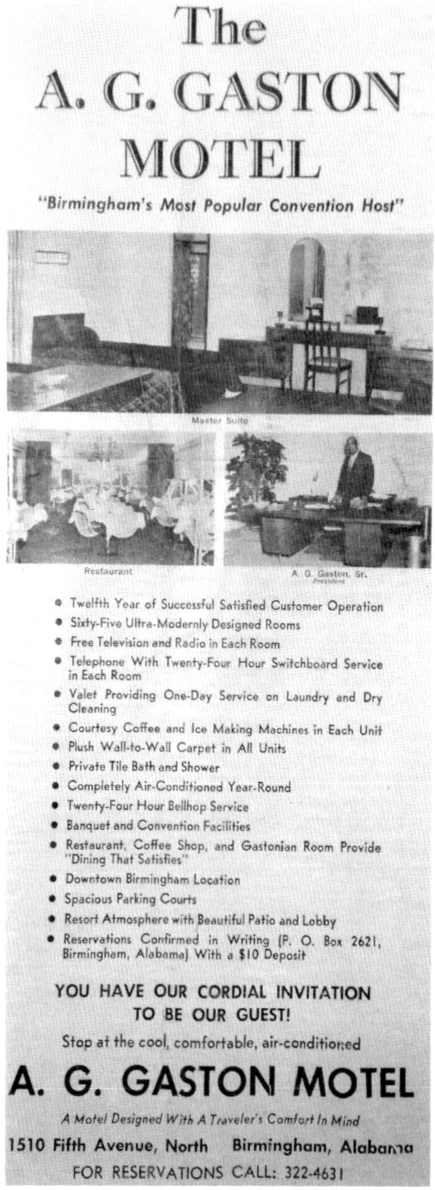

Advertisement for the A.G. Gaston Motel. *Courtesy of Birmingham Civil Rights Institute.*

The place had gone through several expansions since opening in 1954, from housing thirty-two single and double units to forty-eight and then sixty-five. Free TV and radio were added to each room, as were courtesy coffee and ice-making machines. There was a twenty-four-hour switchboard and bellhop service and one-day service on laundry and dry cleaning. And now, it was air conditioned year round. Advertising beckoned, "Stop at the cool, comfortable, air-conditioned A.G. Gaston Motel."

Throughout the years, management continued to go through various changes. Skipwith became the manager, as did Carlton "Sargent" Patton, who led the place in later years. "He was retired from the military and walked around with a gun. He was a security person for Gaston and always carried a big bankroll. He loaned you five dollars, you paid him back ten," Washington said.

At the same time, Gaston was always thinking of ways to draw people in. One day, he called a local musician into his office to help with the next big idea.

John Springer, who was thirty-nine years old at the time, was summoned into Gaston's office. The man talked to Springer about the idea of his performing during the weekends. Springer, who played the bass, had been a musician in the navy and taught music at different schools around the city.

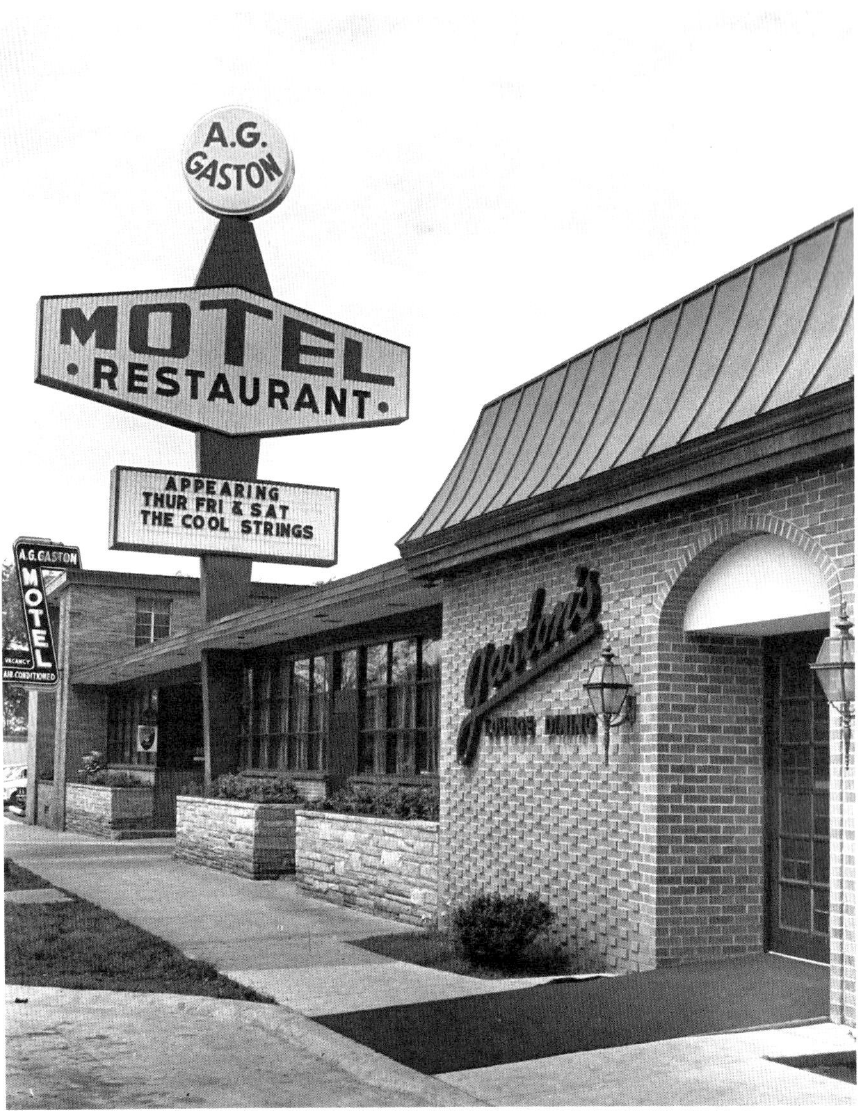

The Gaston Motel. *Photo by Chris McNair of Chris McNair Studios.*

Springer loved the idea and approached fellow musicians Fletcher "Hootie" Myatt, a vocalist and drummer; and Alfonzo Bogus, a pianist, to join him. The Cool Strings trio was born. The men became the official house band for the motel, performing contemporary jazz and a lot of Frank Sinatra. Their music was described as "cool" and "light" by Springer. That's how they got their name.

They performed "music while you dine" on Thursday and Saturday nights, kicking off on August 12, 1965. The men were a hit among the crowd, Springer said. "It was just about the only thing you could go to for something live like that," he said of the motel. "We dressed admirable, considerable, didn't have anyone who had their hair all hanging down."

Gaston nicknamed Springer "Mr. Musician." The men would often play in between sets and even be joined on stage by guest performers who would play the lounge. Every time he came to the motel, Springer said he was surprised by who would come through the doors: jazz alto saxophonist Cannonball Adderley; pianist Ike Cole; baritone bass singer Arthur Prysock and his brother Red Prysock, a tenor saxophonist; jazz pianist Ramsey Lewis; and jazz instrumental ensemble Young Holt Unlimited, to name a few.

Springer remembered that once Arthur Prysock, who was known for hits that included "I Didn't Sleep a Wink Last Night," came without a band, so he asked the Cool Strings to back him up. It was a treat, he said.

Several local musicians wanted a chance to perform with Springer and his band. "We had one fella who wanted to jam with us. He sounded pretty good the first night, so I said come back the rest of the week." Springer agreed to pay the man and let him join along.

"That second night, though, when he came back from the break, he was so drunk, he fell off the stage," Springer remembered. Springer kept playing while the man lay in a stupor on the floor. When it was time for a break, he dealt with him. "I said, 'I tell you what, when you are able to handle your drink, let me know. Until then, see ya.'"

That was the end of him.

One of the perks to performing was that you got a chance to eat in the restaurant, Springer said. "Did I eat there?" he asked with a hungry grin. "Sometimes I would leave home early in time to eat. I would carry my wife and children there when I wasn't playing. The food was good."

Springer said he would often stop by to eat breakfast with Gaston. "Mr. Musician, what you want?" Springer said Gaston would always ask. "I would say, 'Egg and sausage.'"

The men would chat while Gaston read the newspaper. Gaston read the *Wall Street Journal* religiously. Then when he would finish, he'd get up and leave.

Springer remembered that Gaston was a tough man. He and his vice-president, Kirkwood Balton, were discussing some changes to the bar area, and Springer tried to offer some input and was quickly reprimanded. "I said something, and Gaston said, 'Mr. Musician, when I want your word, I will send for it,'" Springer recalled. "That's him. You don't get mad. You accept it. In other words, he was saying, 'I pay this man to make the decisions. I didn't ask you.'"

"Dr. Gaston was real smart," Springer said. "He said the right thing at the right time. Don't cross him."

After a while, Springer added new performers to the band: a new piano player, Willie Cole Smith, and alto saxophonist Charles Clark. From time to time, local soul and gospel artist Roszetta Scofield Johnson would sing with the band. "She was really good and recorded some albums that were popular overseas," Washington remembered. In 1970, Johnson had a Billboard Hot 100 hit with "A Woman's Way."

"That was our entertainment," said Washington of sitting in the lounge taking in the jazz music and the regulars. "We weren't looking at the historical aspect.

"I had a tab there," Washington said. "I paid them at the end of the month and the first of the month just like I paid the white folks. People thought I didn't have to pay because I was related to Gaston, but that was not the case, especially when I started drinking beer and liquor. They wouldn't give that away."

While hanging out at the lounge, Washington remembered when singer Gloria Lynne—famous for her hits "I Wish You Love" and "Speaking of Happiness"—performed one night and they had an exchange. "I was sitting at the bar with her and having a drink," he said. She autographed one of her albums and gave it to Washington. He mistakenly dropped it behind one of the booths and has not seen it since.

Many big-name superstars would perform locally at large venues but lodge and hang out at the motel. Samuetta Drew remembers one Sunday when she and her sister were at the motel. They had been to a concert to hear the Four Tops. One of the group members walked into the lounge and started flirting with her older sister. "That was how it was," she said. "You would be eating there and could run into just about anyone."

Long remembers hearing countless groups at the lounge like the "Queen of Memphis Soul," Carla Thomas, and tenor saxophonist Eddie Harris out of Chicago. According to the *Birmingham News*,[122] former guests included Harry Belafonte, Nat King Cole, Aretha Franklin, Count Basie and Duke Ellington. "Dad and I used to slip in and hear them play," Long said.

The Gaston was also still the place to have your social event, said Bob Dickerson—the place to have dinner after prom, etc. He remembers that his high school football banquet was held there in 1967. He also remembers that after graduating from college, he could go to the lounge. He saw the Commodores perform there. "That was the place during that time," Dickerson said.

My parents, Marvin and Brenda Jones, had their wedding reception there. The 1971 Christmas Eve wedding was celebrated with festive colors. The groomsmen wore tomato red crushed velvet tuxedos with seafoam green shirts. The bride's mother, Jimmie Elliott, ordered a champagne fountain to add to the gaiety. The ornate spout gurgled with bubbly drink and was tempting to the young kids, who thought it was soda. After slipping drink after drink, several of them were tipsy and had to call it an evening.

With segregation outlawed, lots of competition began to pop up, not just from the surrounding black businesses but also from the white businesses that were opening their doors.

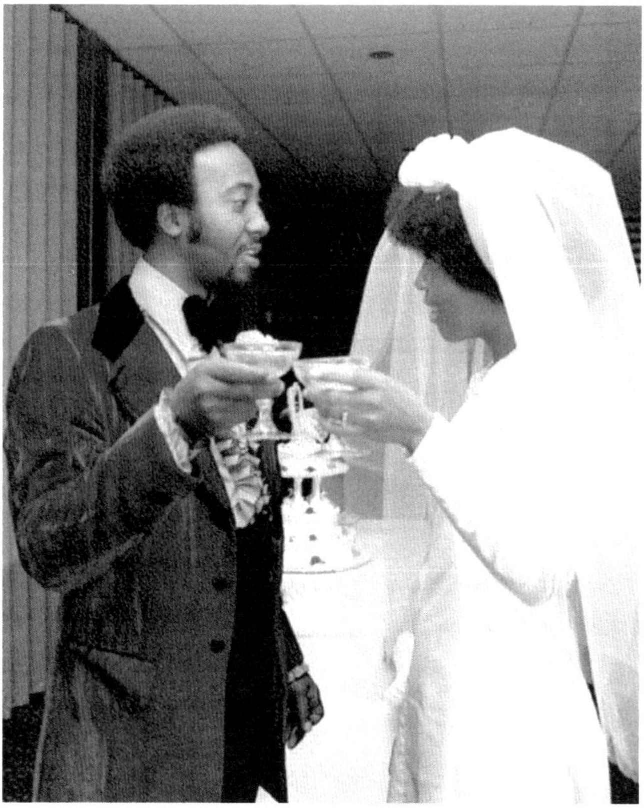

The wedding reception of Marvin and Brenda Jones. *Courtesy of Brenda Jones.*

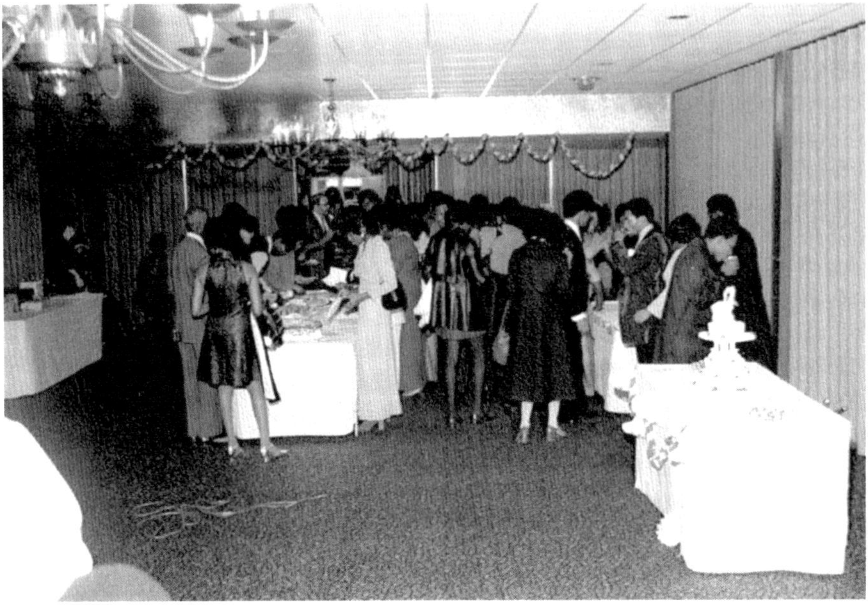

Courtesy of Brenda Jones.

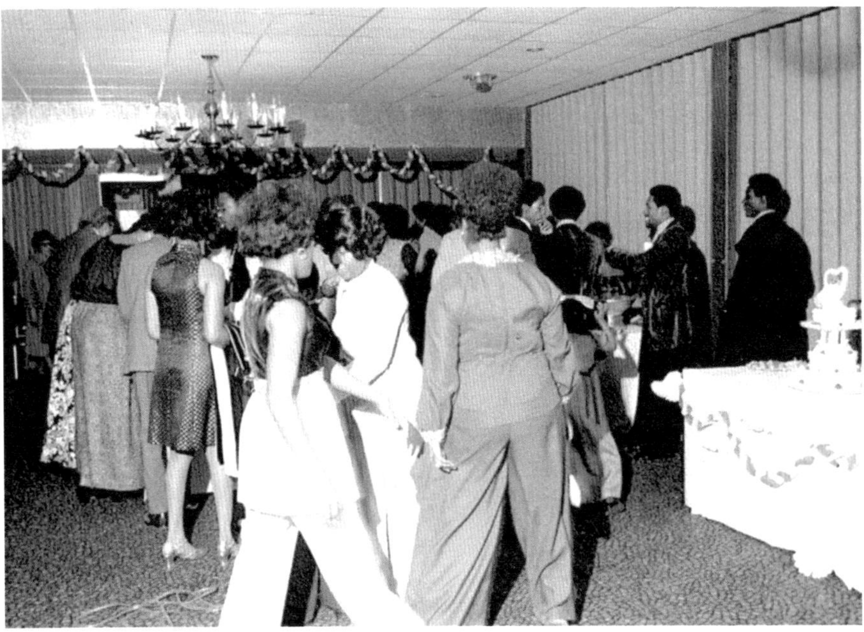

Courtesy of Brenda Jones.

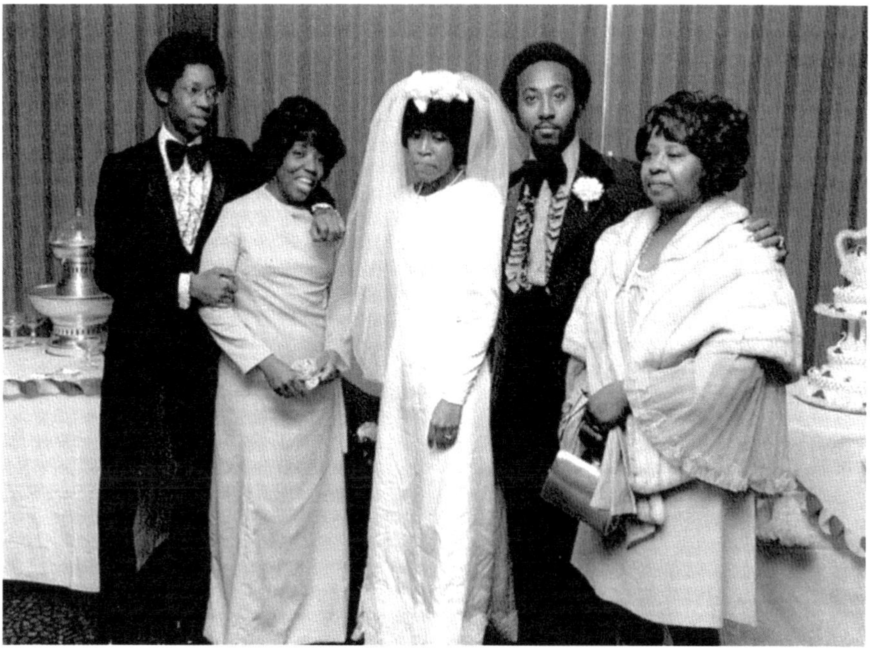

This page: Courtesy of Brenda Jones.

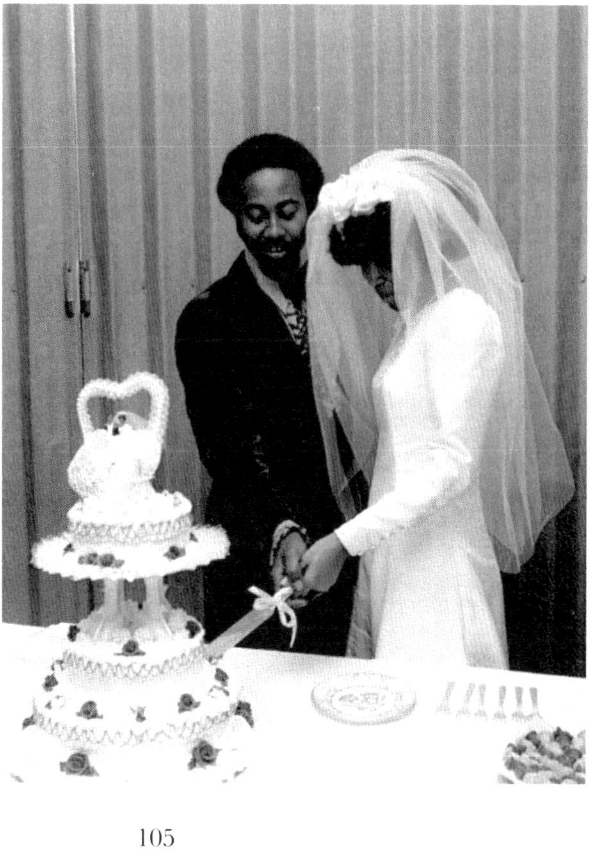

Springer and his band left around 1970. He said that "somebody told Balton to get a rock band."

"I was disappointed that once integration happened it turned into a disco," Long said. "For it to be such an elegant place, I resented that it turned into a disco."

Chapter 10

OUT OF PLACE

By the 1970s, blacks had gained access to more education and better jobs and, therefore, began a slow ascent up the corporate ladder. The big downtown businesses and corporations started to open their doors and offer several African Americans professional positions, including some management roles.

As a result, the Gaston Motel, with its rich history and central location, became the place many of these workers could go for refuge and to be among their own. During lunchtime and happy hour, it was buzzing with black professionals, according to George A. Washington.

"Younger blacks were just starting to move into professional positions at some of the larger corporations in town," said Brenda Faush, who was among them. She worked at Alabama Power Company, which was a leader in hiring African American professionals in Birmingham, she said. There was a group of black professionals who referred to themselves as BAPCO, which stood for Black Alabama Power Company employees, she said. This was the first group of folks who were hired into professional-level positions.

"It was weird," she said of working in that role during the early days. "You would walk through the halls and go through the break rooms, and people would look at you as if you had two heads. They had never seen black professionals."

So, after hours, Faush and the others all fled to the Gaston "as a way to survive what was going on at the corporation and from the employees who were not used to associating with blacks in those settings," she said. "It was not a formalized group, and it was an underground thing," she said. "It was a way to support and strengthen each other when we were not necessarily celebrated at that time."

Shelley Millender recalled that time, too. He was one of the first full-time black automobile salesmen in the Birmingham area and a regular at the motel. He often came with his contemporaries with a mission to get a reprieve from the stressors and stares from the outside community, he said.

"All of these pseudo-elite would congregate at Gaston's," he said. Millender later went on to work at Coca-Cola and would come into the Gaston lounge with his colleagues, who would sport their red jackets, a signature of the company's professionals.

The area teachers and school administrators also had their after-hours spot at the Gaston. They unofficially called themselves the "Coffee Club," said Charles Townsend, a retired principal who frequented the place.

The teachers, whose workday ended at 3:30 p.m., would be the first to get to the motel lounge, Townsend said. The Coffee Club members weren't drinking coffee, though, he said with a laugh. It was usually a stronger drink. They would come in, drink beers and argue about politics.

Across the street at the Gaston-owned urban radio station WENN, the local deejays would beeline over to the Gaston. "A lot of the WENN radio deejays would come in between shows to have a drink," Washington said. One of the popular ones was known for setting a timer in between song sets, getting drunk and then stumbling back into the studio in time to get back on the air, Washington recalled.

"The Gaston complex was the hub for a lot of folks," Faush said. "They would all come from different walks of communities. These days, it seems farfetched that people would all come to one place where they felt they could go feel celebrated and feel like they belong. That one place, the motel, served as that anchor."

As it had been in the past, on any given day, you would see the best and brightest of Birmingham's black community enjoying the music, food and fellowship of the Gaston. But as the years stretched toward the 1980s, with lots of competition for food, music and lodging, business began to slow.

The downfall of the motel, according to *Black Titan: A.G. Gaston and the Making of a Black American Millionaire* by Carol Jenkins and Elizabeth Gardner Hines, "was a result of one of the most profound effects of the civil rights movement...With the end of segregation blacks were free to take their business anywhere they chose, and to the detriment of the black business community, many black citizens chose to spend their money where they could get the best deals—which was more often than not in white-owned stores, whose larger financial bases and backing generally allowed them to offer deeper discounts and broader selection than their black competitors."

Reverend Don Solomon agreed. "The closer we got to integration, the less we [blacks] became the residents of the motel," he said.

"Holiday Inn and everybody else said, 'Come on, we ready for you. Everything is lovely,'" Solomon said. "Gaston just became a competitor trying to get some people in there; everything was wide open then. We went straight to everywhere, except the motel."

"Eventually, it became unprofitable," he said. "When an opportunity came to be considered first class like the rest of the folks, we naturally went to the rest of the folk. That is what happens when you come out of the cotton field; you cannot help yourself," Solomon said. "You go where the bright lights are. No one wants to stay near the cotton fields."

Gaston would remark on how the customers just disappeared, Solomon said. "They didn't go out of town; they were around the corner."

Millender agreed. "We lost a lot in the transition and did not know how well we had it, and by then we could not get it back," he said, referring to a time when black businesses thrived because all they had was one another.

"We used to be called by another name. Then our dollar started counting, and they started calling us 'Mister,'" he said. "Right then, I knew something was funny, wrong."

Also, tourism to the city took a hit, according to *Black Titan*. People were reluctant to visit Birmingham after its international reputation for past civil unrest.[123] So management attempted to call it quits. "But it was the only business that tried to go out of business and couldn't," said Washington. "The loyal customers wouldn't let it close. They kept coming."

A group of the faithful few patrons would come daily to watch the evening news in the lounge, he said. One day, someone broke into the motel and stole the TV. "Management wouldn't replace it," Washington said. But the regular customers would not be defeated. "We got together and bought a TV," Washington said.

"They were trying to quit," he said of the management. "They were looking at the books. They weren't making the kind of money they thought they should."

"It went on like that for a long time," he continued. "Eventually, they just locked the door."

Then one day, a newspaper article announced the motel's fate and an attempt at being reinvented. "A.G. Gaston Motel and Lounge has been an institution in the black business district for almost three decades...Changing times have rendered it virtually useless," wrote Jeff Hardy on Tuesday, December 14, 1982, in the *Birmingham News*.

"We are officially out of the restaurant, motel and bar business," said Louis Willie, executive director of Booker T. Washington Insurance Company, the entity that managed the property. "It is no longer profitable and we decided to convert it to its highest and best use. We are businessmen we decided and it would be foolish to hang onto the hotel for sentimental reasons when it could be used for something useful."

The company invested half a million dollars to make the motel into thirty-nine two-bedroom apartments for the elderly and handicapped. A contract was signed with the Birmingham Housing Authority to take applications. The rent for the residents could be subsidized by the city through the Section 8 Moderate Rehabilitation program. Each unit included a living room, kitchen, bedroom and bath. The popular lounge was converted into a community area. A plaque in the room where Dr. King stayed would be the only reminder of the motel's past, Willie said.

In response to the closing, Birmingham resident Dr. Hattie Bryant Greene wrote to the *Birmingham News* on November 17, 1982:

> *One can't help bemoan the news of the closing of the A.G. Gaston Motel as it opens its doors now for the handicapped. Ever the man to be mindful of those who are less fortunate, Dr. A.G. Gaston has set the type of example which projects the Christian spirit.*
>
> *One looks back over the years and remembers the many affairs, especially those of a religious and social nature, which I have had the honor to organize at the motel—when we, as a Negro race, had no place else to go.*
>
> *It was with pride after the opening that we could journey into other cities and boast of our first-class motel owned and operated by one of our people. It gave us a sense of belonging...Here was the first motel in Birmingham in which Negroes could live. When groups didn't have the means to cover all expenses of their out-of-town guests, we just had to say to Dr. Gaston "...will you look out for them at your place?" The answer was always, "Send them on."*[121]

And it seemed the loss was greater than the motel, Millender pointed out. "Not only did we lose Gaston's, I don't know of any black grocery stores," he said. "We had a lot of black-owned restaurants downtown, record shops, sewing machine repair shops, dress shops. We have a very pronounced absence of black businesses in this area. We didn't cling to those jobs or positions we were forced to have."

Eventually, the apartments for the elderly shut their doors, too. The City of Birmingham acquired ownership, and the motel has sat vacant for many

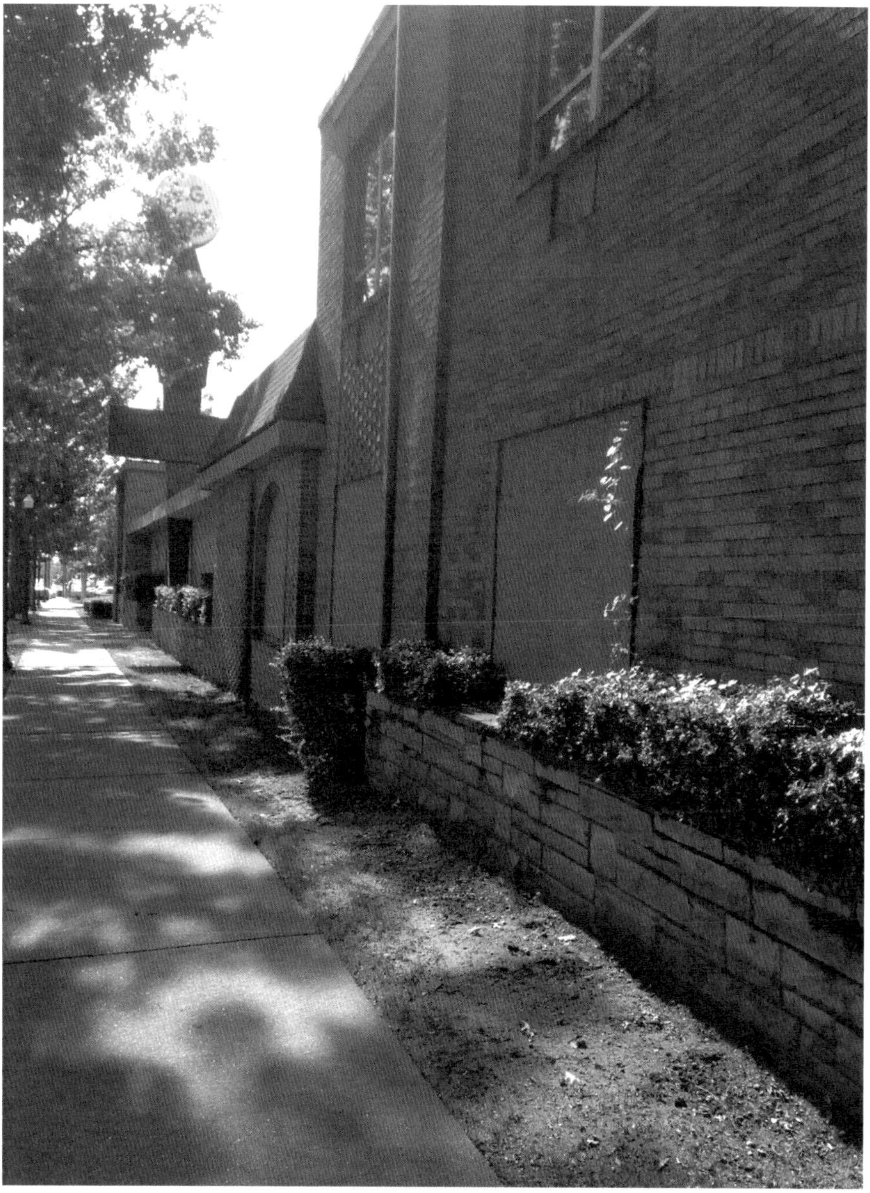

A present-day photo of the A.G. Gaston Motel. *Courtesy of the author.*

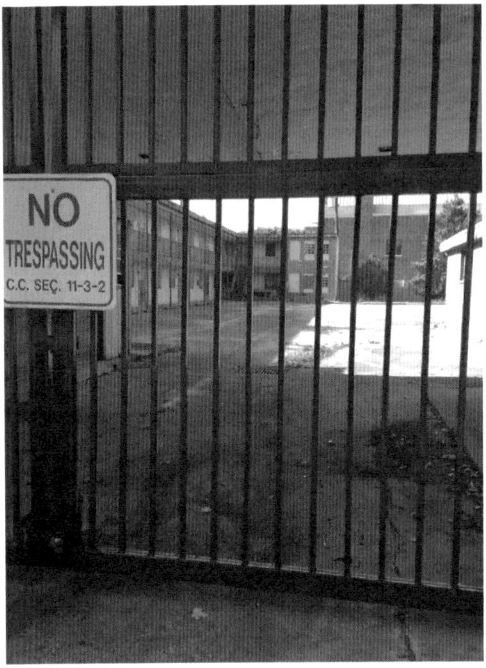

Courtesy of the author.

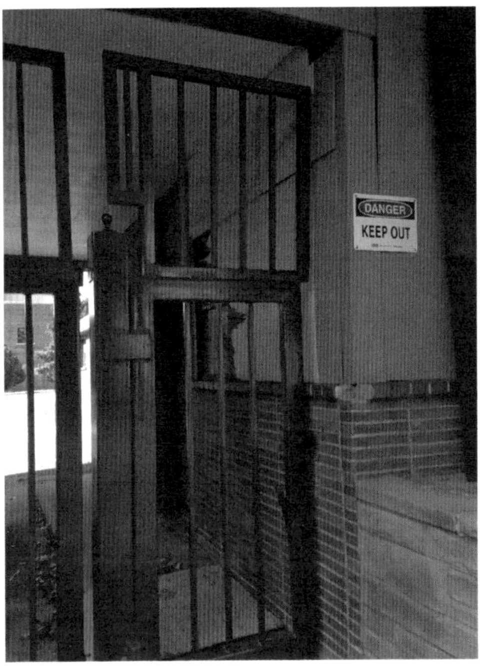

Courtesy of the author.

years, with some attempts to revive it.

According to media reports in 2003, the Birmingham Civil Rights Institute announced plans to take the hotel and expand on its facility, but those were shelved. In 2007, St. Louis developer Michael V. Roberts proposed a $40 million project that would include an upscale hotel, retail space, meeting area and lofts. In this plan, he would have made the motel an interactive museum to complement the BCRI, a concept similar to the National Civil Rights Museum. William Bell, who was a city councilor at the time, supported the plan, but an agreement was never reached with then-mayor Bernard Kincaid.

In 2012, Bell, who became Birmingham mayor, gave the A.G. Gaston Construction Company the task of evaluating the motel's redevelopment opportunities in what is now the city's civil rights district. This was in advance of a planned 2013 yearlong commemoration of the 1963 Birmingham movement. The company was to study the area and present redevelopment options and had volunteered its efforts

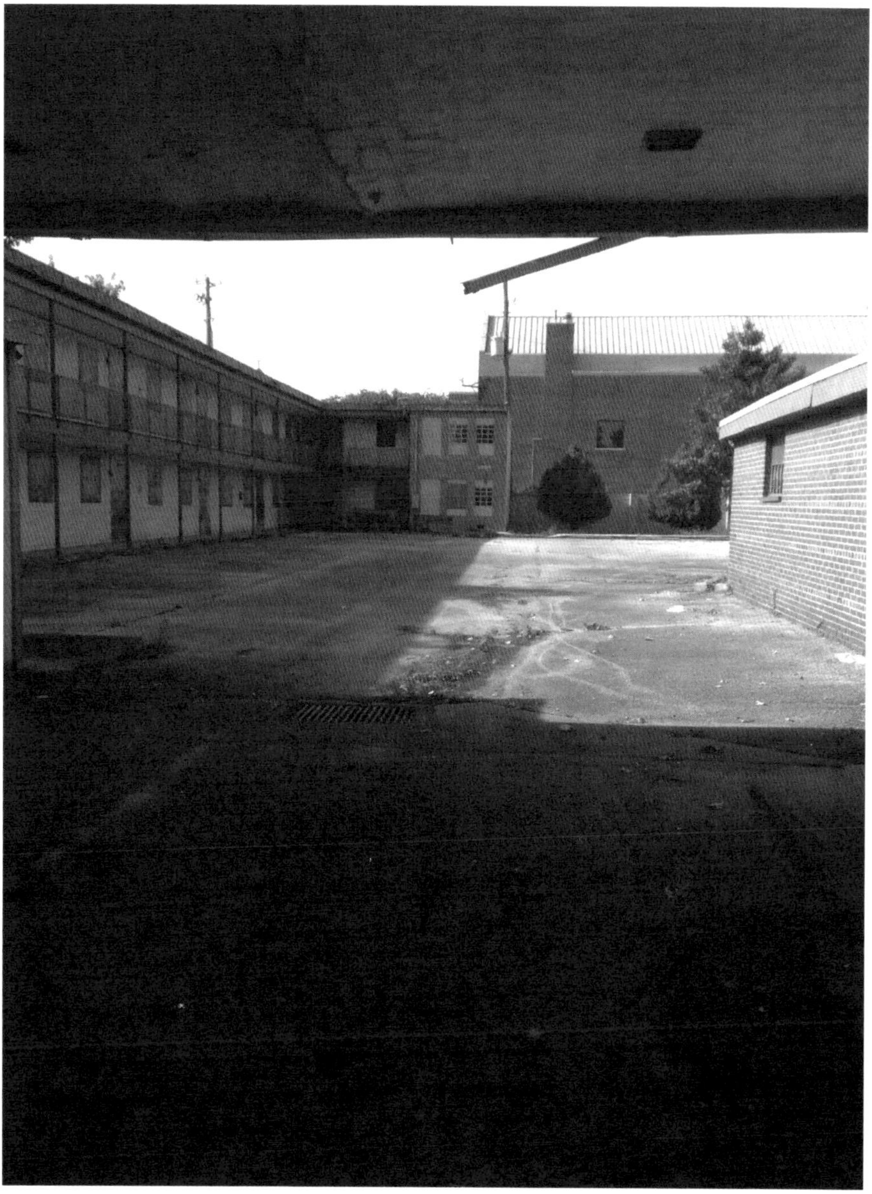

Courtesy of the author.

to do so. According to the *Birmingham News*, however, a report was supposedly due in three months and nothing manifested.[125]

In 2013, Birmingham remembered the pivotal events of 1963 with a year of commemorative events. The city spent at least $600,000 for

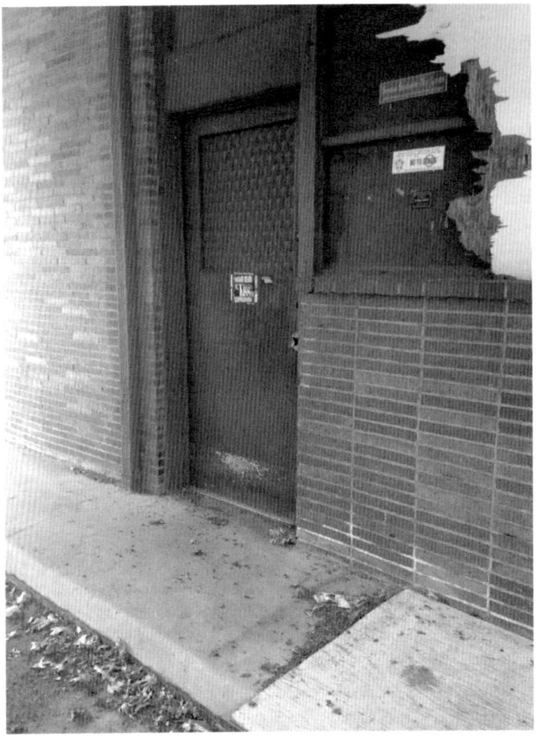

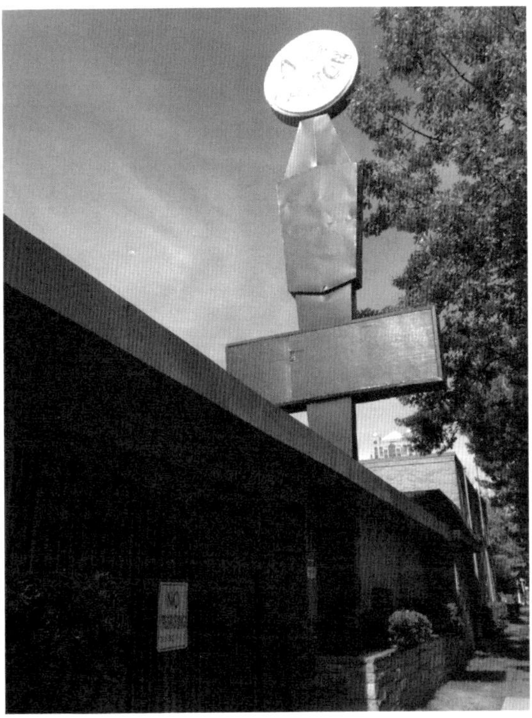

commemoration-related elements, which included two new monuments at Kelly Ingram Park, civil rights trail signs and funding to Miles College and Sixteenth Street Baptist Church. Yet the motel languished. "A.G. Gaston Motel: Civil Rights Era Landmark a Deteriorating Relic Overlooked in 50th Anniversary Fanfare" read a headline in the *Birmingham News*. Critics wondered why, during all the celebrations, the motel still sat abandoned. A graffiti artist vandalized the motel the month the article was published.

Birmingham city councilman Johnathan Austin, in whose district the motel sits, told the media that the city should preserve the motel just as city government requires citizens to keep up their private properties. His fellow councilman Steven Hoyt said it is disgraceful that nothing is being done.

This page: Courtesy of the author.

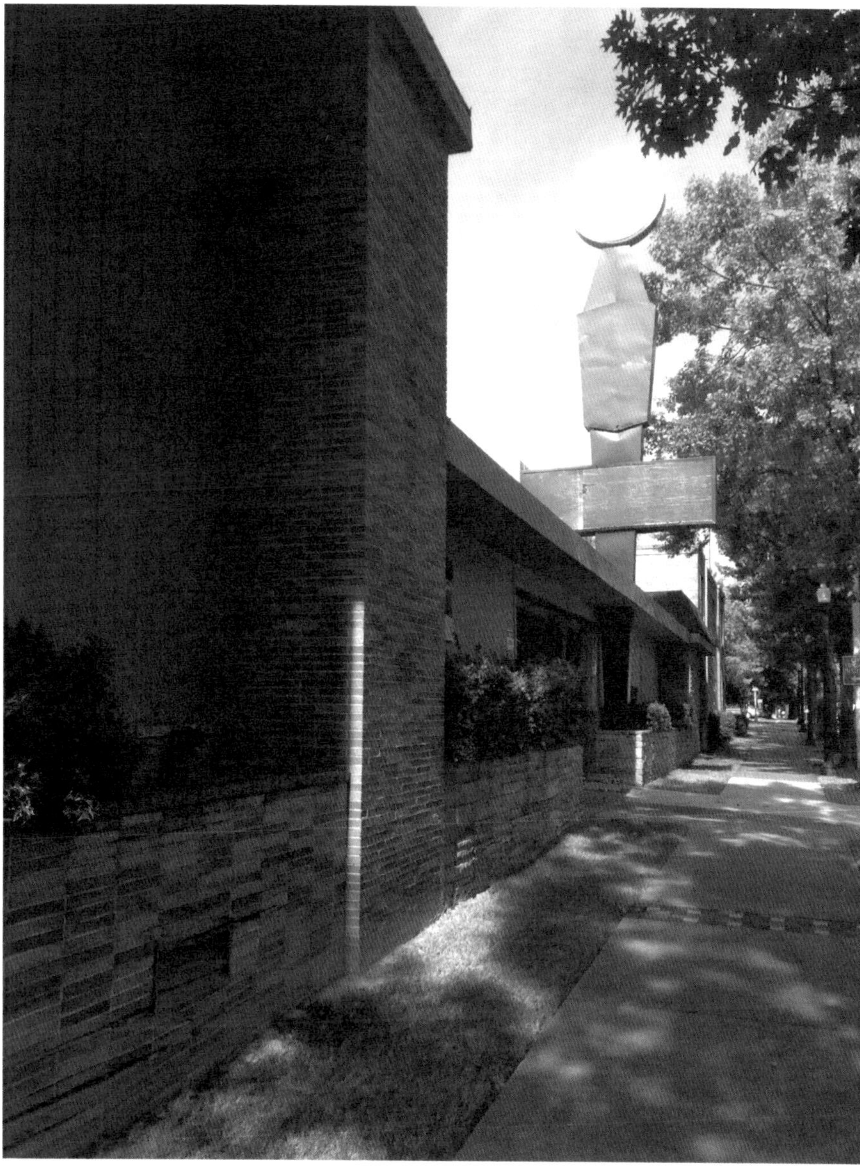

Courtesy of the author.

Hoyt called the decaying motel a "symbol of the city's indifference toward less-glamorous elements that require real attention. While the city's history is celebrated this year, a significant portion of it languishes in neglect," he told local media.

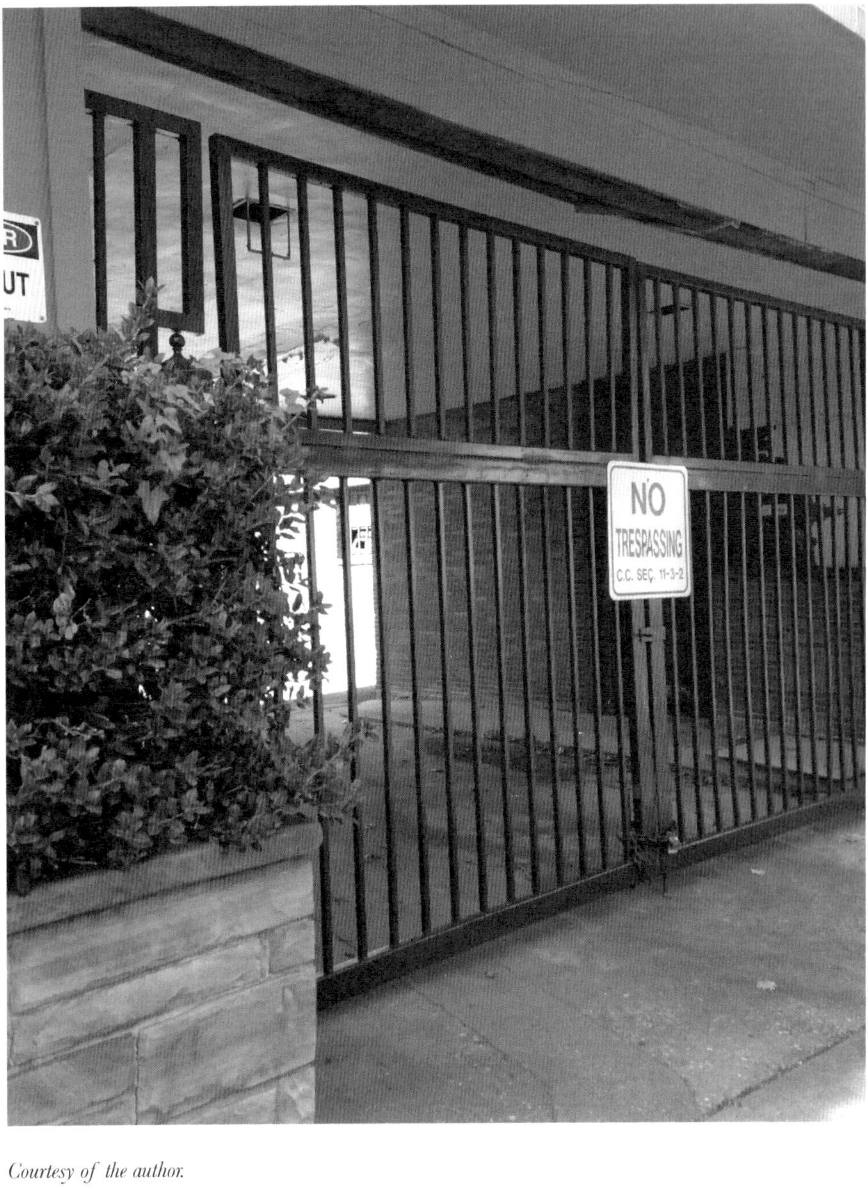

Courtesy of the author.

Today, many passersby do not even notice the place as they zoom along Fifth Avenue North. It has become invisible. A place that once was a symbol, jumping with sound and movement, is now unnoticed and seemingly forgotten. Talks continue, as they have in the past, about doing something with the motel. Until then, it sits.

TIMELINE

July 4, 1892	A.G. Gaston is born.
1939	Booker T. Washington Business School opens.
June 1948	Kiddieland opens.
August 1951	A.G. and Minnie Gaston attend the Methodist conference in Oxford, England.
May 17, 1954	*Brown v. Board of Education*
June 22–27, 1954	Sunday school convention.
July 1, 1954	Gaston Motel officially opens.
1955	Fred Shuttlesworth leads a petition to demand the city hire its first black policeman.
August 28, 1955	Emmett Till is lynched.
1956	Autherine Lucy is admitted to the University of Alabama.
May 20, 1956	Officers padlock the door to the NAACP office.
June 4, 1956	Alabama Christian Movement for Human Rights is founded.
1956	Monday mass meetings begin.
September 2, 1957	Judge Edward Aaron is kidnapped and castrated by the Ku Klux Klan.
1957	Paul R. Jones leases his restaurant at the motel.
1958	Alexander Long begins working as night manager of the motel.
1959	Kirkwood Balton is chosen to oversee operations at the motel.
February 1962	The Miles College selective buying campaign commences.

1962	The $1.5 million A.G. Gaston Building opens.
August 25, 1962	Colin Powell and his wife, Alma, spend their honeymoon at the motel.
September 25–28, 1962	SCLC convention is held in Birmingham.
1962	The Smith and Gaston Funeral home moves.
1962	Townsend opens its Gulf service station.
1962	Paul Jones leaves the motel.
January 1963	Ernest and Carolyn Gibson begin to manage the motel.
1963	Outgoing Alabama governor John Patterson appoints Gaston to the Tuskegee Board of Trustees.
March 15–17, 1963	The Links, Inc. hosts its Southern Area Links gathering.
April 16, 1963	Dr. Martin Luther King Jr. writes "Letter from a Birmingham Jail."
May 12, 1963	The motel is bombed.
May 15, 1963	The KKK burns two twenty-foot crosses in retaliation of the integration order.
May 18, 1963	Floyd Patterson and Jackie Robinson come to Birmingham to encourage nonviolence.
June 12, 1963	Medgar Evers is murdered.
September 15, 1963	The Sixteenth Street Baptist Church is bombed and four little girls are killed.
1964	The Gibsons leave Birmingham.
1964	The Cool Strings begin performing at the lounge.
1970s	Black professionals like Black Alabama Power Company associates congregate at the motel.
December 24, 1971	Marvin and Brenda Jones hold their wedding reception at the motel.
1983	The motel is converted into rental properties for the elderly and handicapped.
2003	Birmingham Civil Rights Institute plans for the motel are shelved.
2007	A St. Louis developer has a proposal for a $40 million project.
2012	Mayor William Bell appoints a construction firm to evaluate the redevelopment of the motel.

NOTES

Chapter 1

1. Bham Wiki, "Kiddieland Park," www.bhamwiki.com/w/Kiddieland.
2. *Birmingham News*, "Kiddieland, Avondale Park Concert Turn Meccas for 32,000 Persons," June 1948.
3. Birmingham's Racial Segregation Ordinances, xroads.virginia.edu/~public/civilrights/ordinances.html.
4. According to Pamela Sterne-King, professor of history at the University of Alabama at Birmingham.
5. Jenkins and Hines, *Black Titan*, 38.
6. Birmingham Historical Society newsletter, November 2012.
7. Bham Wiki, "Collegeville," www.bhamwiki.com/w/Collegeville.
8. From an interview with Hattie Bryant, Urban Impact, a group that serves the interests of the historic black business district.
9. Bham Wiki, "Pythian Temple," www.bhamwiki.com/w/Pythian_Temple.
10. Bham Wiki, "Little Savoy Café," www.bhamwiki.com/w/Little_Savoy_Cafe.
11. Young, *Easy Burden*, 206.
12. Jenkins and Hines, *Black Titan*, 4.
13. Ibid., 141.
14. Ibid., 18.
15. Gaston, *Green Power*, 17.
16. Jenkins and Hines, *Black Titan*, 59.
17. Ibid., 35.
18. Ibid., 71.
19. Ibid., 72.
20. Ibid., 76.
21. Ibid., 78.
22. Gaston, *Green Power*, 60.

23. Jenkins and Hines, *Black Titan*, 132.
24. Ibid., 155.
25. Ibid., 156.
26. Ibid., 157.
27. Ibid., 51.

CHAPTER 2

28. Gaston, *Green Power*, 86.
29. Jenkins and Hines, *Black Titan*, 158.
30. Gaston, *Green Power*, 86.
31. Ibid.
32. Jenkins and Hines, *Black Titan*, 87.
33. Gaston, *Green Power*, 88.
34. Ibid., 91.
35. Ibid., 90.
36. Ibid., 88.
37. Jenkins and Hines, *Black Titan*, 160–61.
38. Young, *Easy Burden*, 229.
39. *The Negro Traveler's Green Book* (Spring 1956).
40. Gaston, *Green Power*, 93.
41. Ibid., 92.
42. Ibid., 93.
43. Ibid., 94.
44. Jenkins and Hines, *Black Titan*, 163.
45. Gaston, *Green Power*, 93.
46. Eskew, "Classes and the Masses," 37.

CHAPTER 3

47. Jenkins and Hines, *Black Titan*, 120.
48. Ibid., 168.
49. White and Manis, *Birmingham Revolutionaries*, 34.
50. Fallin, *African American Church*, 146.
51. White and Manis, *Birmingham Revolutionaries*, 34.
52. Andersen and Thomas, *Living Art*, 145.
53. Ibid.
54. Ibid.
55. Ibid.
56. White and Manis, *Birmingham Revolutionaries*, 34
57. Jenkins and Hines, *Black Titan*, 172.
58. White and Manis, *Birmingham Revolutionaries*, 35.
59. Ibid., 36.
60. Ibid., 37.
61. Ibid.
62. Jenkins and Hines, *Black Titan*, 184.

63. Ibid., 172.
64. White and Manis, *Birmingham Revolutionaries*, 38.
65. Ibid., 43.

CHAPTER 4

66. Jones, oral history, 20.
67. Ibid.
68. Ibid.
69. Jenkins and Hines, *Black Titan*, 176–77.
70. Ibid., 176.
71. Ibid., 188.
72. Ibid., 188.
73. Ibid., 189.
74. Ibid., 190.
75. Andersen and Thomas, *Living Art*, 80.

CHAPTER 5

76. King, *Why We Can't Wait*, 15.
77. "George Wallace's 1963 Inaugural Address," en.wikipedia.org/wiki/George_Wallace's_1963_Inaugural_Address.
78. *Birmingham World*, February 20, 1963.
79. Bham Wiki, "Birmingham Campaign," www.bhamwiki.com/w/Birmingham_Campaign.
80. Abernathy, *And the Walls*, 238.
81. White and Manis, *Birmingham Revolutionaries*, 42.
82. King, *Why We Can't Wait*, 122.
83. Abernathy, *And the Walls*, 240
84. White and Manis, *Birmingham Revolutionaries*, 44.
85. Abernathy, *And the Walls*, 240.

CHAPTER 6

86. White and Manis, *Birmingham Revolutionaries*, 44.
87. Jenkins and Hines, *Black Titan*, 199.
88. Abernathy, *And the Walls*, 247.
89. Ibid.
90. "Letter to Martin Luther King," teachingamericanhistory.org/library/document/letter-to-martin-luther-king.
91. Abernathy, *And the Walls*, 248.
92. Ibid.
93. Ibid., 249.
94. King, *Why We Can't Wait*, 79.
95. Ibid., 80–81.
96. Abernathy, *And the Walls*, 249.
97. Ibid.
98. King, *Why We Can't Wait*, 83.

99. Ibid.
100. Eskew, *But for Birmingham*, 222.
101. "Letter from a Birmingham Jail," www.africa.upenn.edu/Articles_Gen/Letter_Birmingham.html.

Chapter 7

102. Jenkins and Hines, *Black Titan*, xii.
103. Young, *Easy Burden*, 229.
104. Ibid., 230.
105. Ibid.
106. *Birmingham World.*
107. Young, *Easy Burden*, 230.
108. Ibid., 231.
109. Ibid., 233.
110. Ibid.
111. Ibid., 234.
112. Gray, "Birmingham Arrests."

Chapter 8

113. King, *Why We Can't Wait*, 127.
114. Ibid.
115. Ibid., 127–28.
116. Ibid., 128.
117. Ibid.
118. Ibid.
119. Ibid., 128–29.
120. Ibid., 130.

Chapter 9

121. *Birmingham World.*
122. *Birmingham News*, November 1, 1982.

Chapter 10

123. Jenkins and Hines, *Black Titan*, 246.
124. Ibid., 163.
125. Bryant, "A.G. Gaston Motel."

BIBLIOGRAPHY

Abernathy, Ralph David. *And the Walls Came Tumbling Down*. New York: Harper & Row, 1989.

Andersen, Margaret L., and Neil F. Thomas. *Living Art: The Life of Paul of Jones, African American Art Collector*. Newark: University of Delaware Press, 2009.

Arnold, Taschereau. "Young Baptists Invade B'ham for Full Week of Studying." *Birmingham World*, June 22, 1954.

Birmingham News. "Nation's Finest All-Negro Motel Opened." June 30, 1954.

———. "Negro Baptist Congress Hears 'Right to Work' Plea." June 23, 1954.

———. "Negro Church Workers Convene Here." June 22, 1954.

Birmingham World. "Named to Tuskegee Institute Board of Director by Retiring Gov. Patterson." January 16, 1963.

Bryant, Joseph G. "A.G. Gaston Motel: Civil Rights Era Landmark a Deteriorating Relic Overlooked in 50th Anniversary Fanfare." May 30, 2013. blog.al.com/spotnews/2013/05/post_935.html.

Eskew, Glenn T. *But for Birmingham: The Local and National Movements in the Civil Rights Struggle*. Chapel Hill: University of North Carolina Press, 1997.

———. "'The Classes and the Masses': Fred Shuttlesworth's Movement and Birmingham's Black Middle Class." In *Birmingham Revolutionaries: The Reverend Fred Shuttlesworth and the Alabama Christian Movement for Human Rights*, edited by Marjorie L. White and Andrew M. Manis. Macon, GA: Mercer University Press, 2000.

Fallin, Wilson. *The African American Church in Birmingham, 1815–1963: A Shelter in the Storm*. New York: Routledge, 1997.

Fazio, Michael W. *Landscape of Transformation: Architecture and Birmingham Alabama*. Knoxville: University of Tennessee Press, 2010.

Gaston, A.G. *Green Power: The Successful Way of A.G. Gaston*. AL: Big City Brands LLC, 2013.

Gray, Jeremy. "Birmingham Arrests Reached 1,500; Joan Baez Performed at Miles College (May 5, 1963)." May 5, 2013. AL.com. blog.al.com/birmingham-news-stories/2013/05/birmingham_arrests_reached_150.html.

Huntley, Horace, and John W. McKerley, eds. *Foot Soldiers for Democracy: The Men, Women and Children of the Birmingham Civil Rights Movement*. Champaign: University of Illinois Press, 2009.

Jackson, Emory O. "Nat'l SS, BTU Congress Opens 49th Session in City Today." *Birmingham World*, June 22, 1954.

Jackson, Richard A. "Baptists Re-elect Doctor Jernagin During SS, BTU Congress." *Birmingham World*, June 22, 1954.

Jenkins, Carol, and Elizabeth Gardner Hines. *Black Titan A.G. Gaston and the Making of a Black American Millionaire*. New York: One World Ballantine Books, 2004.

Jones, Paul R. Oral history, Birmingham Civil Rights Institute.

Kincey, Robert W. "Kiddieland, Avondale Park Concert Turn Meccas for 32,000 Persons." *Birmingham News*, June 1948.

King, Martin Luther, Jr. *Why We Can't Wait*. New York: Penguin Group, Inc., 1963.

McWhorter, Diane. *Carry Me Home Birmingham, Alabama: The Climatic Battle of the Civil Rights Revolution*. New York: Simon & Schuster. 2010.

Patrick Dorsey, Mignette Y. *Speak Truth to Power: The Story of Charles Patrick, a Civil Rights Pioneer*. Tuscaloosa: University of Alabama Press, 2010.

Smith, Suzanne. *To Serve the Living: Funeral Directors and the African American Way of Death*. Cambridge, MA: Belknap Press of Harvard University Press, 2010.

White, Marjorie L., and Andrew M. Manis, eds. *Birmingham Revolutionaries: The Reverend Fred Shuttlesworth and the Alabama Christian Movement for Human Rights*. Macon, GA: Mercer University Press, 2000.

Young, Andrew. *An Easy Burden: The Civil Rights and the Transformation of America*. New York: HarperCollins, 1996.

INDEX

A

Abernathy, Reverend Ralph 50, 64
Adelman, Robert 78
A.G. Gaston Construction Company 112
A.G. Gaston Restaurant 55
A.H. Smith Construction Company 55
Alabama Christian Movement for Human Rights 39, 117
Allen, W.J. 34
Anderson, Dr. W.G. 46, 50
Austin, Johnathan 114

B

Baez, Joan 76, 78
Bell, William 112, 118
Bogus, Alfonzo 100
Booker T. Washington Business College 34, 36, 50
Burnham, Brooke B. 30

C

Clark, Charles 102
Collins, Addie Mae 93
Connor, Eugene "Bull" 66
Cool Strings, the 100, 118

D

Dickerson, Bob 102
Drew, Samuetta Hill 17

E

Echols, Stanley B. 30, 55
Elliott, Jimmie 103

F

Faush, Brenda 15, 107

G

Gardner, Edna 12, 28
Gardner, Reverend W. Edmund 46
Gaston, A.G. 11, 19, 25, 32, 42, 50, 62, 69, 92, 109, 110, 117
Gaston, Creola Smith 22
Gaston, Minnie 11, 28, 117
Gibson, Carolyn 12, 118
Gibson, Ernest 30, 118
Goldsmith, Alliene 34
Goodgame, Reverend J.W. 34

Greene, Dr. Hattie Bryant 110
Green, Victor H. 28
Gregory, Dick 78, 82, 92

H

Hall, L.R. 34
Hanson, Clarence B., Jr. 82
Hester, R.A. 33
Hibbler, Al 66, 76
Hoyt, Steven 114

J

Jackson, Emory O. 65
Jackson, Ruth J. 34
Jenkins, Edwin 25
Jenkins, Elizabeth 25
Jimerson, Norman C. 90
Jimerson, Rand 90
Johnson, Tamara Harris 11, 17
Jones, Brenda 103, 118
Jones, Marvin 103
Jones, Paul R. 42, 48, 117

K

Kennedy, Bobby 76, 94
Kennedy, President John F. 72, 82
Kiddieland Park 15
Kincaid, Bernard 112
King, Dr. Martin Luther, Jr. 32, 89
King, Reverend A.D. 88, 92

L

Long, Dale 36, 63, 67, 78, 91
Long, Ken 93
Lucy, Autherine 39, 117

M

Mabry, Jesse 40
Mathis, Johnny 76
Matthews, Samuel 18
McKinstry, Carolyn 27, 35
McNair, Chris 12, 93
McNair, Denise 93
McNair, Maxine 93
Millender, Shelley 45, 50, 108
Monk, Mary Means 18
Morgan, James W. 32
Mullins, Clarence 18
Myatt, Fletcher "Hootie" 100

P

Patton, Carlton "Sergeant" 99
Peevy, T.A., Jr. 96
Pitts, Lucius 46

R

Rayfield, Wallace 18
Robertson, Carole 93
Robinson, Jackie 28, 46, 48, 76, 92, 118
Ruth, Mamie 31

S

Scofield Johnson, Roszetta 102
Shores, Arthur Davis 18
Shuttlesworth, Reverend Fred 117
Sixteenth Street Baptist Church 12, 35, 39, 50, 71, 93, 114, 118
Skipwith, Arzell "Skippy" 37
Small, George C. 30
Smith, Willie Cole 102
Smyer, Sid 45
Solomon, Reverend Don 23, 29, 109
Southern Christian Leadership Conference 45, 46
Springer, John 90, 99
Steel City Construction Company 12, 30
Sterne, Mervyn H. 33
Stewart, Shelley 43, 67, 82

T

Townsend, Charles 108
Tuggle, Carrie "Granny" 21

W

Walker, Wyatt Tee 46, 76, 86
Wallace, Governor George 54
Washington, Booker T. 80
Washington, George A. 12, 18, 96, 107
WENN radio 108
Wesley, Cynthia 93
Wilkins, Roy 75, 77
Windham Construction Company 19

Y

Young, Reverend Andrew 19, 27, 75, 76, 77

ABOUT THE AUTHOR

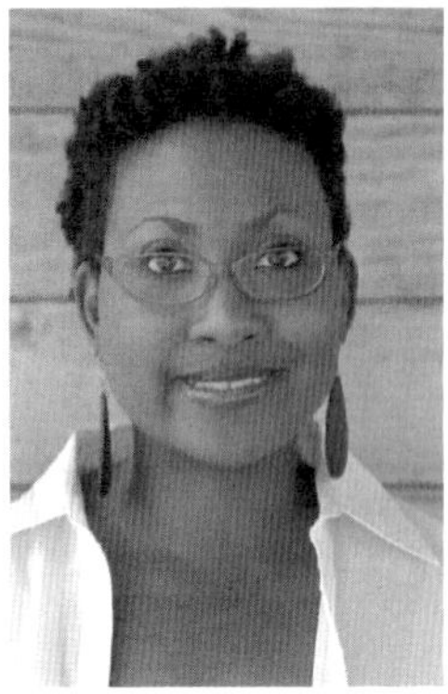

Marie A. Sutton is an award-winning freelance writer with a passion for immortalizing the African American experience. She has worked as a journalist, communications professional, radio talk show host and blogger. She is currently the director of student media at the University of Alabama at Birmingham. She lives in Birmingham, Alabama, with her devoted husband, James, and two beautiful children, Simone and Stephen.